HAMMOND

Family Reference

WORLD ATLAS

DOUBLEDAY & COMPANY, INC.

GARDEN CITY   NEW YORK

Contents

GAZETTEER-INDEX OF THE WORLD

Country	Area (Square Miles)	Population	Index Ref.	Plate No.
Afars and Issas, Terr. of....	8,498	125,050	P 9	63
Afghanistan	250,000	15,751,000	A 2	48
Africa	11,682,000	311,000,000		62–65
Alabama, U.S.A.	51,609	3,462,000		104–105
Alaska, U.S.A.	586,400	253,000		106–107
Albania	11,100	1,965,000	E 5	35
Alberta, Canada	255,285	1,463,203		96–97
Algeria	919,591	12,540,000	G 5	62
American Samoa	76	29,000	K 7	56
Andaman & Nicobar Is., India	3,215	63,548	G6–7	49
Andorra	175	14,000	G 1	27
Angola (Port.)	481,351	5,293,000	K14	64
Antarctica	5,500,000			11
Antigua and Dependencies (Br.)	171	60,000	G 3	77
Antilles, Greater and Lesser	91,122	22,948,000	D 3	76
Arabia	1,200,000	14,310,000	D 5	44
Argentina	1,072,068	23,031,000		70
Arizona, U.S.A.	113,909	1,608,000		108–109
Arkansas, U.S.A.	53,104	1,960,000		110–111
Armenian S.S.R., U.S.S.R.	11,506	2,194,000	F 6	37
Ascension, I., St. Helena....	34	476	D13	64
Asia	17,032,000	1,884,695,000		42–43
Australia	2,974,581	12,000,000		58–59
Australian Capital Terr.	939	103,573	H 7	59
Austria	32,374	7,322,700	B 3	32
Azerbaidzhan S.S.R., U.S.S.R.	33,436	4,660,000	G 6	37
Azores, Portugal	893	327,480	B 4	62
Bahama Islands (Br.)	4,404	144,000	C 1	76
Bahrein	231	195,000	F 4	44
Balearic Islands, Spain	1,936	443,327	H 3	27
Barbados	166	244,962	G 4	77
Belgium	11,779	9,606,000	C 6	20
Bermuda (Br.)	21	51,000	G 2	77
Bismarck Arch., Terr. New Guinea	18,770	224,964	E 6	56
Bolivia	424,163	3,801,000	G 7	68
Botswana	219,815	593,000	L16	65
Brazil	3,286,473	85,655,000		69,71
British Columbia, Canada....	366,255	1,873,674		98–99
British Honduras	8,867	113,000	B 1	78
British Indian Ocean Terr.	58.3	2,000	L10	43
Brunei	2,226	104,000	E 4	54
Bulgaria	42,829	8,309,000	G 4	34
Burma	261,789	25,811,000	A 2	53
Burundi	10,747	3,340,000	N12	65
California, U.S.A.	158,693	18,602,000		112–113
Cambodia	69,898	6,415,000	D 4	53
Cameroon	183,568	5,493,000	J10	62
Canada	3,851,809	20,700,000		84–85
Canal Zone (U.S.A.)	553	55,600	E 3	79
Canary Islands, Spain	2,808	944,448	B 4	26
Cape of Good Hope, S. Afr.	262,079	3,936,306	L18	65

Country	Area (Square Miles)	Population	Index Ref.	Plate No.
Cape Verde Is. (Port.)	1,557	228,000	N 5	9
Caroline Is., Terr. Pacific Is.	367	52,166	E 5	56
Cayman Is. (Br.)	100	9,000	B 3	76
Celebes, Indonesia	72,986	6,288,043	G 6	55
Central African Republic ..	240,534	1,459,000	K10	63
Central America	196,928	14,628,000		78–79
Ceylon	25,332	11,741,000	E 7	49
Chad	495,753	3,500,000	K 8	63
Channel Is. (Br.)	75	115,000	E 6	17
Chatham Is., N. Z.	372	520	J10	56
Chile	292,257	8,780,000		70
China (mainland)	3,691,506	732,000,000		50–51
China (Taiwan)	13,948	13,700,000	K 7	51
Christmas I., Aust.	52	3,381	O11	43
Cocos Is., Aust.	5.4	684	N11	43
Colombia	439,513	19,215,000	F 3	68
Colorado, U.S.A.	104,247	1,969,000		114–115
Comoro Is. (Fr.)	838	244,000	P14	65
Congo, Democratic Republic of the	905,536	16,210,000	L12	65
Congo, Rep. of	132,046	1,000,000	J12	64
Connecticut, U.S.A.	5,009	2,832,000		116–117
Cook Is. (N. Z.)	93	19,251	K 7	56
Corsica, France	3,368	275,465	A 6	25
Costa Rica	19,575	1,610,000	E 5	79
Crete, Greece	3,218	483,075	G 8	35
Cuba	44,206	8,074,000	B 2	76
Curaçao, Neth. Antilles	182	134,250	E 4	77
Cyprus	3,473	614,000	E 5	46
Czechoslovakia	49,370	14,305,000	D 2	32
Dahomey	44,290	2,514,000	G10	62
Daito Is., Ryukyu Is.	17	3,896	M 6	51
Delaware, U.S.A.	2,057	505,000		139
Denmark	16,614	4,900,000	E 9	19
District of Columbia, U.S.A.	69	803,000	B 5	138
Dominica (Br.)	290	69,000	G 4	77
Dominican Republic	18,704	3,889,000	D 3	77
Ecuador .... approx.	109,483	5,508,000	E 4	68
Egypt (U.A.R.)	386,100	30,907,000	M 6	63
El Salvador	8,260	3,151,000	C 4	78
England, U.K.	50,327	45,680,870		17
Equatorial Guinea, Spain....	10,832	277,000	H11	62,64
Estonian S.S.R., U.S.S.R. ..	17,413	1,285,000	C 3	36
Ethiopia	471,776	24,581,027	O 9	63
Europe	4,063,000	620,890,000		14–15
Faerøe Is., Den.	540	38,000	D 2	14
Falkland Is. (Br.)	4,618	2,000	H14	71
Fernando Po, Eq. Guin.	786	76,000	H11	62
Fiji (Br.)	7,015	490,000	H 7	56
Finland	130,128	4,700,000	O 5	18
Florida, U.S.A.	58,560	5,805,000		118–119
France	212,841	50,000,000		24–25
French Guiana	35,135	37,000	K 3	69
French Polynesia	1,544	98,400	M 7	56

Country	Area (Square Miles)	Population	Index Ref.	Plate No.
Gabon	103,346	473,000	J12	64
Gambia	4,003	343,000	C 9	62
Georgia, U.S.A.	58,876	4,357,000		120–121
Georgian S.S.R., U.S.S.R.	26,911	4,548,000	F 6	37
Germany, East (German Democratic Republic)	41,814	17,067,000		22–23
Germany, West (Federal Republic of)	95,959	59,948,500		22–23
Ghana	91,843	8,400,000	F10	62
Gibraltar (Br.)	2	25,000	D 4	26
Gilbert & Ellice Is. (Br.)	369	55,000	H 6	56
Great Britain & Northern Ireland (United Kingdom)	94,214	55,068,000		16–17
Greece	50,548	8,716,000	F 6	35
Greenland (Den.)	840,000	43,000	B12	10
Grenada (Br.)	133	97,000	G 6	77
Guadeloupe and Dependencies (Fr.)	687	320,000	F 3	77
Guam (U.S.A.)	212	94,000	E 4	56
Guatemala	42,042	4,717,000	B 3	78
Guinea	94,925	3,702,000	D 9	62
Guyana	83,000	645,098	J 2	69
Haiti	10,694	4,674,000	D 3	76
Hawaii, U.S.A.	6,424	711,000		122
Holland (Netherlands)	13,958	12,668,000	E 4	20
Honduras	43,277	2,445,440	D 3	78
Hong Kong (Br.)	398	3,900,000	J 7	51
Hungary	35,915	10,241,000	E 3	33
Iceland	39,768	200,000	C 2	14
Idaho, U.S.A.	83,557	692,000		123
Ifni, Spain	579	53,000	D 6	62
Illinois, U.S.A.	56,400	10,644,000		124–125
India	1,283,166	515,777,000		48–49
Indiana, U.S.A.	36,291	4,885,000		126–127
Indonesia	575,893	112,311,000		54–55
Iowa, U.S.A.	56,290	2,760,000		128–129
Iran	636,293	26,315,000	F 3	45
Iraq	167,924	8,380,000	D 3	44
Ireland	26,600	2,884,002	B 4	17
Israel	7,993	2,716,000		47
Italy	116,303	53,700,000		28–29
Ivory Coast	124,503	4,000,000	E10	62
Jamaica	4,411	1,880,000	C 3	76
Japan	142,734	100,300,000		52
Java, Indonesia	48,842	60,909,381	K 2	55
Jordan	37,737	2,123,000		47
Kansas, U.S.A.	82,264	2,234,000		130–131
Kazakh S.S.R., U.S.S.R.	1,048,301	12,129,000	G 5	38
Kentucky, U.S.A.	40,395	3,179,000		132–133
Kenya	224,960	10,300,000	O11	65
Kirghiz S.S.R., U.S.S.R.	76,641	2,652,000	H 5	38
Korea, North	46,540	12,400,000	C 2	52
Korea, South	38,452	30,067,000	C 3	52
Kuwait	6,177	491,000	E 4	44
Laccadive, Minicoy & Amindivi Is., India	746	24,108	C6,7	49
Laos	91,459	2,800,000	D 3	53
Latvian S.S.R., U.S.S.R.	24,595	2,263,000	B 3	36
Lebanon	4,015	2,460,000	F 6	46
Lesotho	11,716	877,000	M17	65
Liberia	43,000	1,115,000	E10	62
Libya	679,359	1,800,000	K 6	62–63
Liechtenstein	61	20,000	J 3	31
Lithuanian S.S.R., U.S.S.R.	25,174	2,986,000	B 3	36
Louisiana, U.S.A.	48,523	3,534,000		134–135
Luxembourg	999	335,000	H 8	20
Macao (Port.)	6.2	280,000	H 7	51
Madeira Is., Portugal	308	268,937	A 2	26
Maine, U.S.A.	33,215	993,000		136–137
Malagasy Republic	226,657	6,400,000	R15	65
Malawi	45,483	4,042,412	N14	65
Malaya, Malaysia	50,670	8,415,000	C 7	53
Malaysia	128,308	9,906,000	C–F 4	54
Maldive Islands	115	100,883	L 9	43
Mali	463,948	4,745,000	E 9	62
Malta	122	315,765	E 7	29
Man, Isle of (Br.)	227	50,423	D 3	17
Manitoba, Canada	251,000	963,066		92–93
Mariana Is., Terr. Pac. Is.	184	10,743	E 4	56
Marquesas Is., Fr. Poly.	492	4,837	N 6	56
Marshall Is., Terr. Pac. Is.	70	18,239	H 4	56
Martinique (Fr.)	425	330,000	G 4	77
Maryland, U.S.A.	10,577	3,519,000		138–139
Massachusetts, U.S.A.	8,257	5,348,000		140–141
Mauritania	397,954	1,100,000	D 8	62
Mauritius	709	790,000	S19	65
Mexico	761,601	45,671,000		80–81
Michigan, U.S.A.	58,216	8,218,000		142–143
Midway Is. (U.S.A.)	2	2,355	H 3	56
Minnesota, U.S.A.	84,068	3,554,000		144–145
Mississippi, U.S.A.	47,716	2,321,000		146–147
Missouri, U.S.A.	69,686	4,497,000		148–149
Moldavian S.S.R., U.S.S.R.	13,012	3,368,000	C 5	37
Monaco	368 acres	23,000	G 6	25
Mongolia	604,247	1,140,000	E–H 2	50–51
Montana, U.S.A.	147,138	706,000		150–151
Montserrat (Br.)	38	14,000	G 3	77
Morocco	171,834	14,140,000	E 5	62
Mozambique (Port.)	302,328	7,124,000	O15	65
Muscat and Oman	82,000	565,000	G 5	26
Natal, S. Afr.	33,578	2,979,920	N17	65
Nauru	8.2	6,056	G 6	56
Nebraska, U.S.A.	77,227	1,477,000		152–153
Nepal	54,362	10,294,000	E–F 3	49
Netherlands	13,958	12,668,000	E 4	20
Netherlands Antilles	394	212,000	E 4	77
Nevada, U.S.A.	110,540	440,000		154
New Britain, Terr. New Guinea	14,098	154,188	F 6	56
New Brunswick, Canada	28,354	616,788	C 3	86
New Caledonia (Fr.)	7,335	92,000	G 8	56
Newfoundland, Canada	156,185	493,396	J 4	86
New Guinea, Terr. of (Aust. Trust.)	92,160	1,582,439	E–F 6	56
New Hampshire, U.S.A.	9,304	669,000		155
New Hebrides (Br.-Fr. Cond.)	5,700	78,000	G 7	56
New Jersey, U.S.A.	7,836	6,774,000		156–157
New Mexico, U.S.A.	121,666	1,029,000		158–159
New South Wales, Aust.	309,433	4,300,083	H 6	59
New York, U.S.A.	49,576	18,073,000		160–161
New Zealand	103,736	2,747,093	M 7	59
Nicaragua	45,698	1,783,000	E 4	78
Niger	489,189	3,546,000	H 8	62
Nigeria	356,669	61,450,000	H10	62
Niue (N. Z.)	100	5,194	K 7	56
Norfolk I., Aust.	13.3	1,152	G 8	56
North America	9,363,000	294,000,000		74–75
North Carolina, U.S.A.	52,712	4,914,000		162–163
North Dakota, U.S.A.	70,665	652,000		164–165
Northern Ireland, U.K.	5,459	1,491,000	G 3	17
Northern Territory, Aust.	520,280	39,556	E 3	58
Northwest Territories, Canada	1,304,903	28,738	E–J 3	84–85
Norway	125,181	3,800,000	F 6	18
Nova Scotia, Canada	21,425	756,039		86–87
Ohio, U.S.A.	41,222	10,245,000		166–167
Oklahoma, U.S.A.	69,919	2,482,000		168–169
Ontario, Canada	412,582	6,960,870		90–91
Orange Free State, S. Afr.	49,866	1,386,547	M17	65
Oregon, U.S.A.	96,981	1,899,000		170–171
Orkney Is., Scotland	376	18,424	E 1	16
Pacific Is., Terr. of the (U.S. Trust.)	700	93,000	D–G 5	56
Pakistan	365,527	107,258,000	B3,C4	48
Palau Is., Terr. Pac. Is.	179	11,225	D 5	56
Panama	29,209	1,372,200	G 6	79
Papua (Aust.)	86,100	600,597	B 7	54
Paraguay	157,047	2,161,000	J 8	69,71
Pennsylvania, U.S.A.	45,333	11,520,000		172–173
Persia (Iran)	636,293	26,315,000	F 3	45
Peru	496,222	12,385,000	E 5	68
Philippines, Rep. of the	115,707	35,576,000	H 4	55
Pitcairn Is. (Br.)	1.8	96	O 8	56
Poland	120,664	31,944,000		21
Portugal	35,510	9,381,000	B 3	26
Portuguese Guinea	13,948	528,000	C 9	62
Portuguese Timor	5,762	560,000	H 7	55
Prince Edward I., Canada.	2,184	108,535	F 3	87
Puerto Rico	3,435	2,727,000	G 2	77
Qatar	8,500	75,000	F 4	45
Québec, Canada	594,860	5,780,845		88–89
Queensland, Aust.	667,000	1,688,529	G 4	59

Country	Area (Square Miles)	Population	Index Ref.	Plate No.
Réunion (Fr.)	969	418,000	R20	65
Rhode Island, U.S.A.	1,214	920,000		141
Rhodesia	150,332	4,530,000	M15	65
Río Muni, Eq. Guin.	10,046	201,000	J11	64
Rumania	91,699	19,287,000	G 3	34
Russian S.F.S.R., U.S.S.R.	6,592,819	126,561,000	D–R 4	38–39
Rwanda	10,691	3,306,000	N12	65
Ryukyu Is. (U.S. Adm.)	848	952,000	G 4	52
Sabah, Malaysia	29,388	588,000	F 4–5	54–55
St. Christopher-Nevis-Anguilla (Br.)	138	58,000	F 3	77
St. Croix, Virgin Is. (U.S.A.)	80	14,973	H 2	77
St. Helena (Br.)	47	5,125	E15	64
St. John, Virgin Is. (U.S.A.)	20	925	H 1	77
St. Lucia (Br.)	238	99,000	G 4	77
St-Pierre & Miquelon (Fr.)	93.5	5,000	H 6	87
St. Thomas, Virgin Is. (U.S.A.)	32	16,201	G 1	77
St. Vincent (Br.)	150	90,000	G 4	77
Sakhalin, U.S.S.R.	28,215	618,000	P 4	39
San Marino	23.4	18,000	D 2	28
São Tomé e Príncipe (Port.)	372	60,000	H11	64
Sarawak, Malaysia	48,250	903,000	E 5	54
Sardinia, Italy	9,301	1,400,103	B 4	29
Saskatchewan, Canada	251,700	955,344		94–95
Saudi Arabia	920,000	6,870,000	D 4	44
Scotland, U.K.	30,411	5,187,000	D 2	16
Senegal	75,750	3,580,000	D 9	62
Seychelles (Br.)	109	48,000	T 6	9
Shetland Is., Scotland	551	17,719	G 1	16
Siam (Thailand)	198,456	34,800,000	C 3	53
Sicily, Italy	9,926	4,683,076	D 6	29
Sierra Leone	27,925	2,439,000	D10	62
Singapore	225	1,955,600	E 6	53
Society Is., Fr. Poly.	646	68,245	L 7	56
Solomon Is., Terr. New Guinea	4,080	56,000	F 6	56
Solomon Is. Prot. (Br.)	11,500	141,000	G 6	56
Somali Republic	246,200	2,700,000	R11	63,65
South Africa	471,663	18,733,000	L18	65
South America	6,875,000	166,000,000		68–71
South Australia, Aust.	380,070	1,107,178	E 5	58
South Carolina, U.S.A.	31,055	2,542,000		174–175
South Dakota, U.S.A.	77,047	703,000		176–177
Southern Yemen	111,075	1,158,000	E 7	44
South-West Africa (S. Afr.)	317,838	596,000	K16	64–65
Spain	194,896	32,140,036		26–27
Spanish Sahara, Spain	102,702	48,000	D 6	62
Sudan	967,495	14,800,000	M 9	63
Sumatra, Indonesia	164,148	14,982,910	C 6	54
Surinam (Neth.)	55,144	350,000	J 3	69
Svalbard, Norway	23,958	2,828	C 2	18
Swaziland	6,704	374,697	N17	65
Sweden	173,665	7,803,425	J 6	19
Switzerland	15,941	6,025,000		30–31
Syria	71,498	5,450,000	G 5	46
Tadzhik S.S.R., U.S.S.R.	55,251	2,579,000	G 6	38
Tahiti, Fr. Poly.	402	45,430	M 7	56
Taiwan, China	13,048	13,700,000	K 7	51
Tanzania	362,819	12,500,000	N13	65

Country	Area (Square Miles)	Population	Index Ref.	Plate No.
Tasmania, Aust.	26,215	376,212	J 8	59
Tennessee, U.S.A.	42,244	3,845,000		178–179
Texas, U.S.A.	267,339	10,551,000		180–181
Thailand	198,456	34,800,000	C 3	53
Tibet, China	471,660	1,270,000	C 5	50
Togo	5,765	1,746,000	G10	62
Tokelau Is. (N. Z.)	3.9	1,901	J 6	56
Tonga	270	77,429	J 7	56
Transkei, S. Afr.	16,675	1,439,195	M18	65
Transvaal, S. Afr.	109,621	6,273,477	N17	65
Trinidad & Tobago	1,980	1,000,000	G 5	77
Tristan da Cunha, St. Helena	40	285	O 7	9
Trucial Oman	32,278	150,000	F 5	45
Tuamotu Arch., Fr. Poly.	343	7,097	M 7	56
Tunisia	63,378	4,700,000	H 5	62
Turkey	301,381	31,391,421		46
Turkmen S.S.R., U.S.S.R.	188,456	1,914,000	F 6	38
Turks & Caicos Is. (Br.)	166	6,000	D 2	76
Uganda	92,674	7,934,000	N11	65
Ukrainian S.S.R., U.S.S.R.	232,046	45,516,000	D 5	37
Union of Soviet Socialist Republics	8,649,498	253,543,000		36–39
United Arab Republic	386,100	30,907,000	M 6	63
United Kingdom	94,214	55,068,000		16–17
United States of America land	3,554,609			
land and water	3,615,211	200,996,000		102–103
Upper Volta	105,841	5,054,000	F 9	62
Uruguay	72,172	2,783,000	J10	71
Utah, U.S.A.	84,916	990,000		182
Uzbek S.S.R., U.S.S.R.	173,591	10,581,000	G 5	38
Vatican City	109 acres	1,000	B 6	29
Venezuela	352,143	9,415,000	G 2	68
Vermont, U.S.A.	9,609	397,000		183
Victoria, Aust.	87,884	3,271,993	G 7	59
Vietnam, North	61,293	19,500,000	D 3	53
Vietnam, South	66,263	17,000,000	E 4	53
Virgin Is. (Br.)	59	9,000	H 1	77
Virgin Is. (U.S.A.)	133	56,000	H 1	77
Virginia, U.S.A.	40,815	4,457,000		184–185
Wake I. (U.S.A.)	3	1,097	G 4	56
Wales, U.K.	8,017	2,709,930	E 4	17
Wallis & Futuna (Fr.)	106	8,611	H–J 7	56
Washington, U.S.A.	68,192	2,990,000		186–187
Western Australia, Aust.	975,920	863,744	C 4	58
Western Samoa	1,097	135,000	J 7	56
West Irian (Indon. Adm.)	159,371	800,000	J 6	55
West Virginia, U.S.A.	24,181	1,812,000		188–189
White Russian S.S.R., U.S.S.R.	80,154	8,633,000	C 4	37
Wisconsin, U.S.A.	56,154	4,144,000		190–191
World	57,491,000	3,443,000,000		8–9
Wyoming, U.S.A.	97,914	340,000		192
Yap, Terr. Pac. Is.	46	6,606	D 5	56
Yemen	75,000	5,000,000	D 7	44
Yugoslavia	98,766	20,210,000	C 3	34
Yukon Territory, Canada	207,076	14,382	C 3	84
Zambia	290,585	3,947,000	M14	65

THE SOLAR SYSTEM

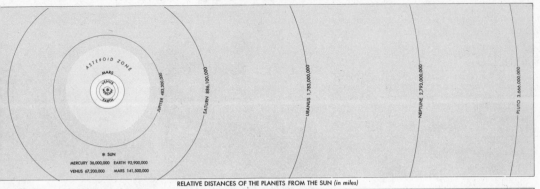

ASTEROID ZONE

MARS
VENUS
EARTH

JUPITER 483,300,000

SATURN 886,100,000

URANUS 1,783,000,000

NEPTUNE 2,793,000,000

PLUTO 3,666,000,000

* SUN

MERCURY 36,000,000 EARTH 92,900,000
VENUS 67,200,000 MARS 141,500,000

RELATIVE DISTANCES OF THE PLANETS FROM THE SUN (in miles)

EARTH
7,927

VENUS
7,575

MARS
4,216

PLUTO
3,600

MERCURY
3,009

URANUS 30,878   NEPTUNE 27,700

JUPITER 88,698

SATURN 75,060

RIM OF SUN

RELATIVE DIAMETERS OF THE PLANETS (in miles)

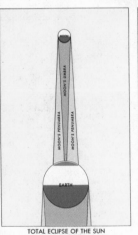

MOON
MOON'S UMBRA
MOON'S PENUMBRA
MOON'S PENUMBRA
EARTH

TOTAL ECLIPSE OF THE SUN

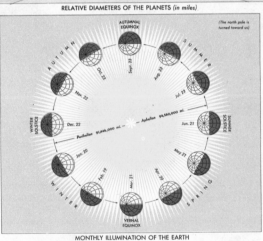

AUTUMNAL
EQUINOX

(The north pole is
turned toward us)

AUTUMN
SUMMER

Oct. 23
Sept. 23
Aug. 23
Jul. 23

Nov. 22
Jun. 21

WINTER SOLSTICE
Dec. 22
Perihelion 91,666,000 mi.   Aphelion 94,560,000 mi.
SUMMER SOLSTICE

Jan. 20
May 21

Feb. 19
Apr. 20

WINTER
Mar. 21
SPRING

VERNAL
EQUINOX

MONTHLY ILLUMINATION OF THE EARTH

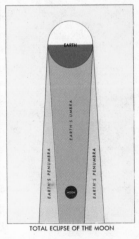

EARTH
EARTH'S UMBRA
EARTH'S PENUMBRA
EARTH'S PENUMBRA
MOON

TOTAL ECLIPSE OF THE MOON

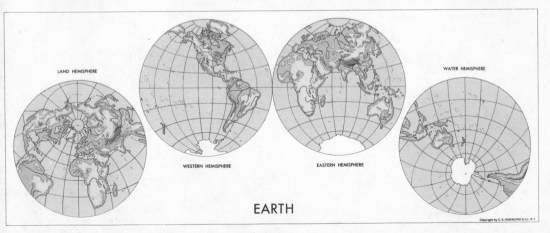

LAND HEMISPHERE

WATER HEMISPHERE

WESTERN HEMISPHERE

EASTERN HEMISPHERE

EARTH

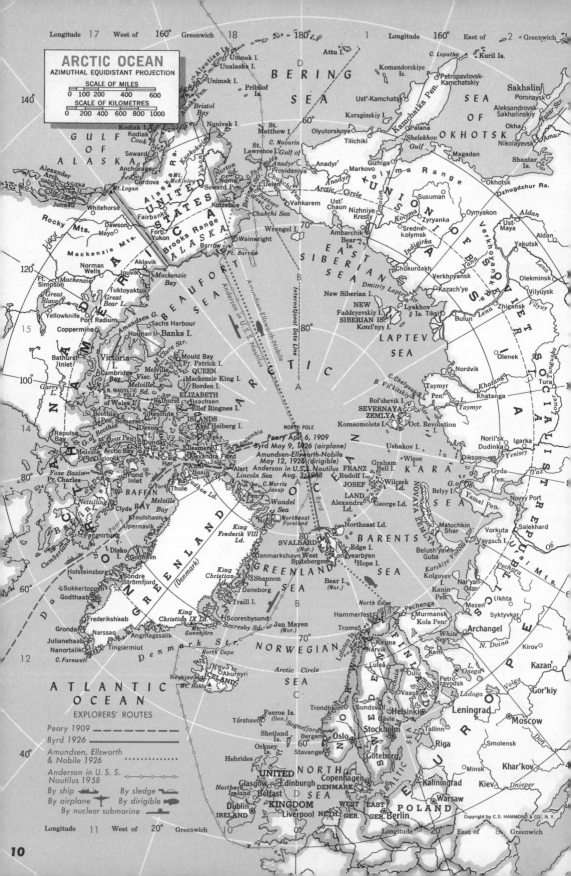

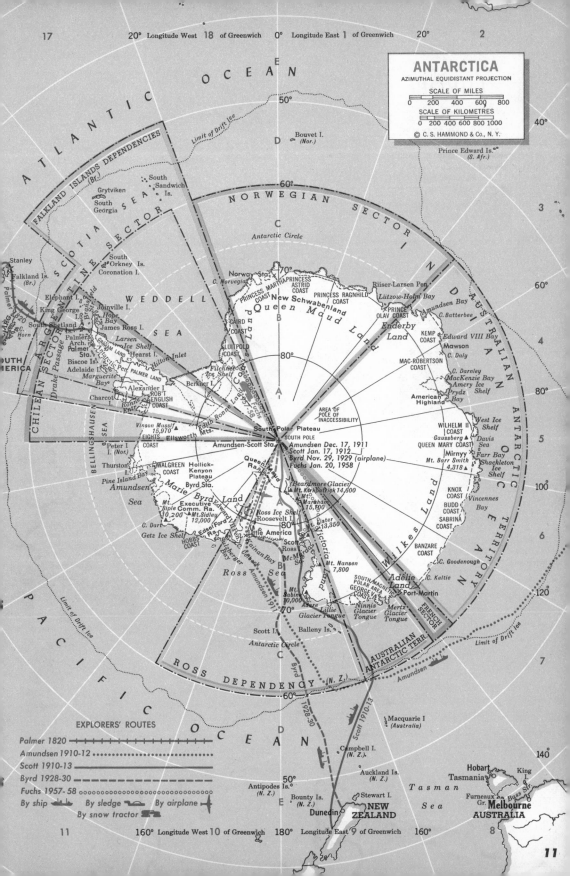

Map of EUROPE

SCALE OF MILES

0   100   200   300   400

✪ Capitals of Countries
• Cities
▬▬▬ Boundaries of Countries
▬▬▬ Other Boundaries
▲ Mountain Peaks

Mountains   Highlands   Lowlands   Depression   Water

ARC

NORWEGIAN SEA

40°   30°   20°   10°   0°

Reykjavik
ICELAND

N O R

Faeroe Islands (Danish)

Shetland Islands (British)

Trondheim

Bergen

Orkney Islands

Oslo

Hebrides

50°

Skagerrak   Kattegat   Göteb

A T L A N T I C   O C E A N

Scotland

Glasgow

NORTH SEA

DENMARK

Copenhagen

Northern Ireland

GREAT

British Isles

IRELAND   IRISH SEA

Dublin

Liverpool

Hamburg

Wales   BRITAIN
England

NETHER-LANDS

EAST Berlin

London

The Hague   Amsterdam

Greenwich

WEST

Brussels

BELGIUM   Bonn   GERMANY

English Channel

Le Havre

LUXEM-BOURG

Frankfurt

Nantes   Seine R.   Paris

Loire River   River

Rhine R.   Danube

CZECH

GERMANY

Bay of Biscay

FRANCE

Munich
LIECHT.

Vienn

40°

Bilbao

Bordeaux

SWITZER-LAND   Bern

AUSTRI

Oporto

PYRENEES

Lyon R.

MT.   Milan   Trieste   Zagreb

Iberian

Rhône R.

Blanc   Po   Venice

Marseille

Genoa   River

ADRIA

Lisbon

PORTUGAL

SPAIN

Madrid

ANDORRA

MONACO

Corsica (French)

SAN MARINO

Cape St. Vincent

Peninsula

Barcelona

Rome

ITALY

Valencia   Balearic Islands (Spanish)

VATICAN CITY

Seville

Sardinia (Italian)

Naples

GIBRALTAR (British)
Strait of Gibraltar

Tangier   Ceuta (Spanish)

Rabat   Melilla (Spanish)

Algiers

Palermo

MEDITERRAN

MOROCCO   ALGERIA   Tunis   Sicily (Italia)

30°

AFRICA   TUNISIA

MALTA

10°   0°   10°

Longitude West of Greenwich

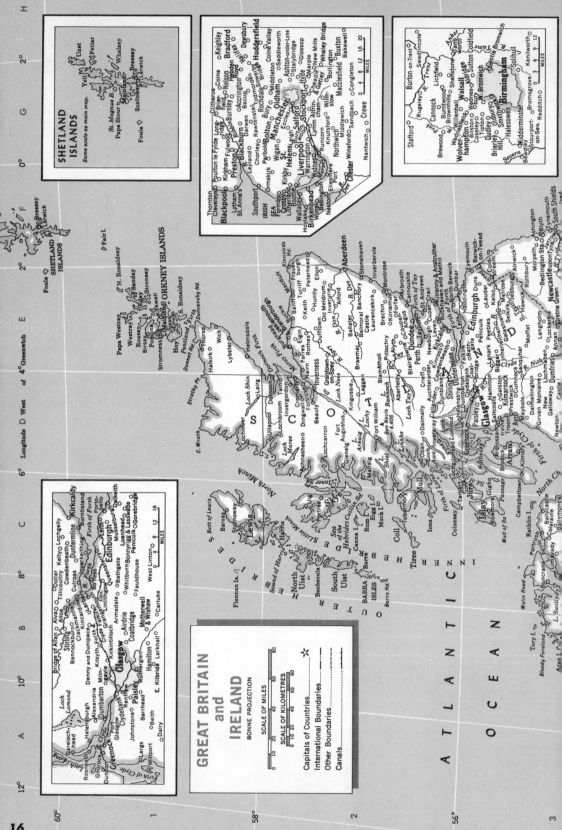

SHETLAND ISLANDS

Same scale as main map.

GREAT BRITAIN
and
IRELAND

BONNE PROJECTION

SCALE OF MILES

SCALE OF KILOMETRES

Capitals of Countries................
International Boundaries.............
Other Boundaries.....................
Canals...................................

ATLANTIC OCEAN

17

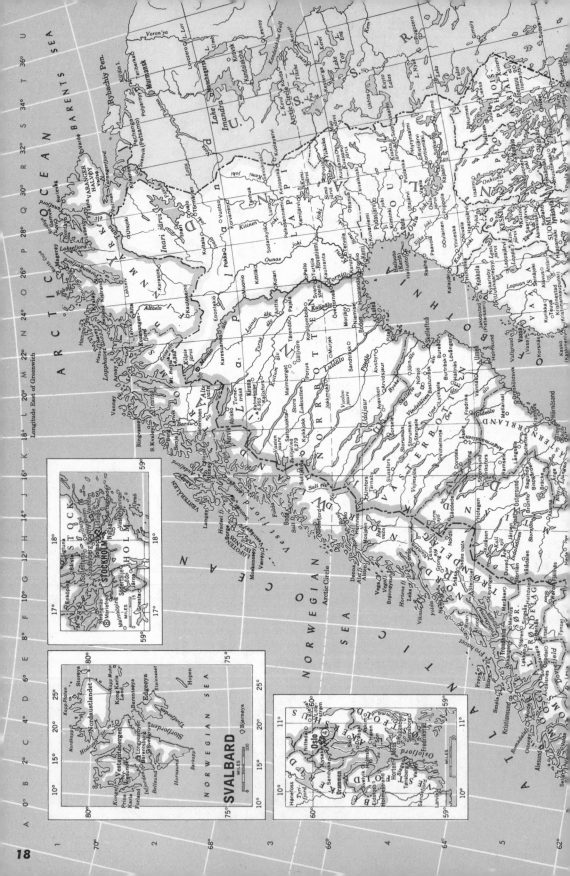

SVALBARD

STOCKHOLM

18

NORWAY, SWEDEN FINLAND and DENMARK

CONIC PROJECTION

SCALE OF MILES

SCALE OF KILOMETRES

Capitals of Countries .... ★
Administrative Centers .... ☆
International Boundaries
Internal Boundaries
Canals

SUBDIVISIONS
Indicated by Numbers
Fylker in NORWAY
1 Akershus   G6
2 Vestfold   G7
3 Østfold   G7
4 Oslo   G7
5 Bergen   D6
Oslo is the administrative center for Akershus and Oslo Fylker; Bergen for Hordaland and Bergen Fylker.

Län in SWEDEN
6 Göteborg och
  Bohus   G7
7 Västmanland   K7
8 Södermanland   K7
9 Östergötland   J7
10 Malmöhus   H9
11 Kristianstad   J8

19

NETHERLANDS, BELGIUM and LUXEMBOURG

CONIC PROJECTION

SCALE OF MILES

KILOMETRES

Capitals of Countries _____ ☆
Provincial Capitals _____ ◉
International Boundaries _____
Provincial Boundaries _____
Canals _____

Copyright by C. S. HAMMOND & Co., N. Y.

20

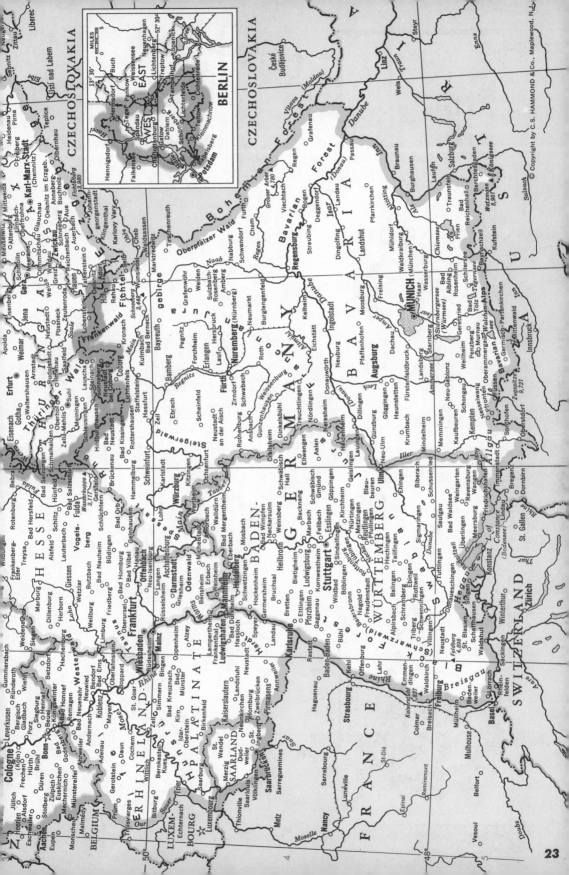

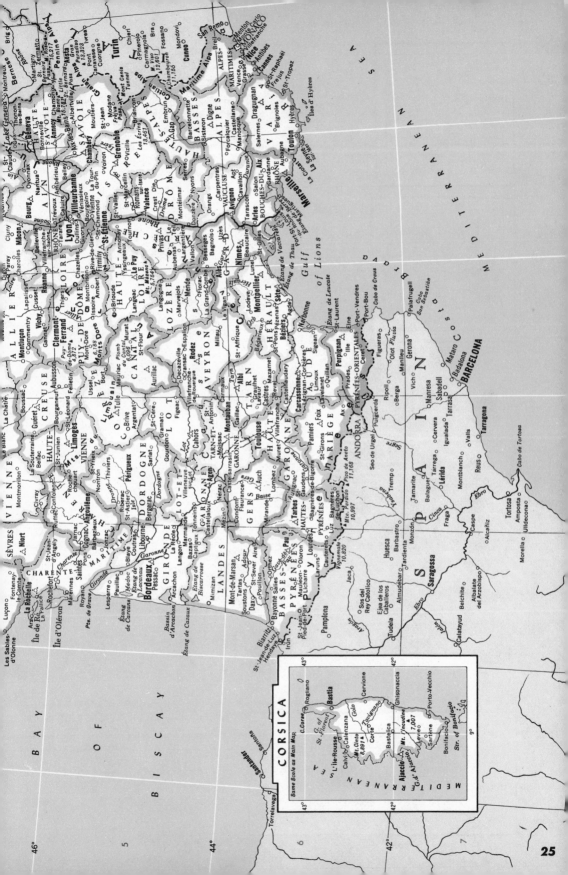

25

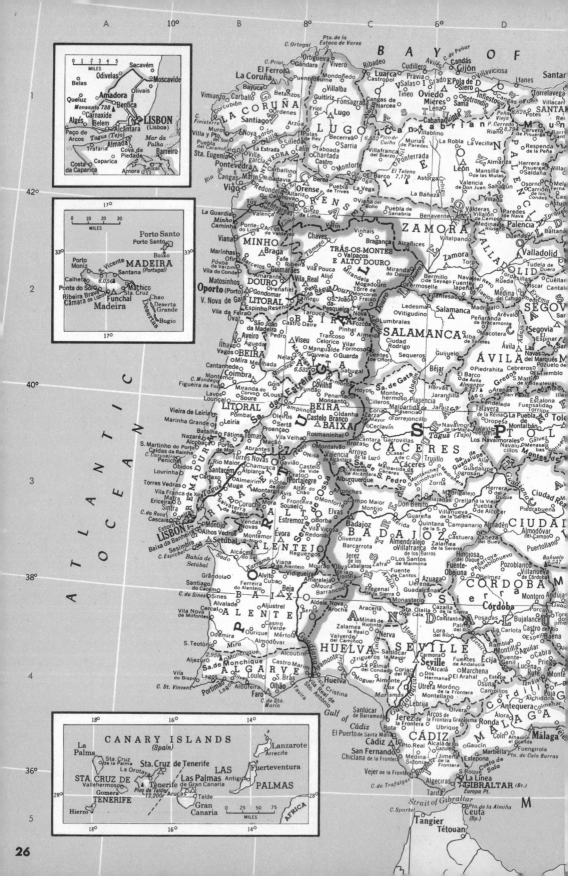

Inset maps

LISBON (Lisboa) inset
0 1 2 3 4 5
MILES

Sacavém
Belas · Odivelas · Moscavide
Queluz · Olivais
Amadora · Benfica
Monsanto 738 ▲
Carnaxide
Algés · Belem
Paço de Arcos · Alcântara
Trafaria · Almada
Cova da Piedade
Costa · Caparica
da Caparica
Amora
Barreiro
LISBON (Lisboa)
Tagus (Tejo)
Mar da Palha

MADEIRA (Portugal) inset
17°
0 10 20 30
MILES
Porto Santo
Porto Santo
Baixo
Porto Moniz
São Vicente
Santana
Calheta · 6.056 ▲ · Mathico
Ribeira Brava · Sta. Cruz
Ponta do Sol · Chao
Câmara · **Funchal** · Deserta Grande
Madeira · Bugio
Deserta
33°

CANARY ISLANDS (Spain) inset
18° 16° 14°
CANARY ISLANDS
(Spain)
La Palma
Lanzarote
Arrecife
Sta. Cruz
de la Palma
La Orotava
Sta. Cruz de Tenerife
LAS · Fuerteventura
STA. CRUZ DE · Las Palmas · Antigua
TENERIFE · de Gran Canaria · **PALMAS**
Vallehermoso · Pico de Teide
Gomera · 12,200 ▲ · Arucas
Tenerife · Telde
Hierro · **Gran Canaria**
0 25 50 75
MILES
AFRICA
28°

Main map — Spain and Portugal

BAY OF

Pta. de la Estaca de Vares
C. Ortegal · C. de Peñas
C. Prior · Ortigueira
El Ferrol · Cudillero · Avilés · Candás · Gijón · Villaviciosa · Llanes · Santan
La Coruña · Vivero · Ribadeo · Luarca · Castropol · Oviedo · Infiesto · Torrelavega · SANTA
Vimianzo · Carballo · Betanzos · Bayuca · Puentedeume · Mondoñedo · Villalba · Tineo · Mieres · Lena · Sama · Sotrondio · 8,628 ▲
Corcubión · Ordenes · Friol · Fonsagrada · Cangas de Narcea · Cabañaquinta · P. Cerredo · 8,794 ▲ · Cervera de Piguerga · Barri
C. Finisterre · Santiago · Arzúa · **LUGO** · Lugo · Villablino · Riaño · Potes · Cerver
Noya · Villa y Pto. del Son · Pta. de los Reyes · Becerreá · 6,552 ▲ · Pico de Cuiña · Murias de Paredes · La Robla · La Vecilla · Mansilla · Respenda de la Peña · Herrera de
Pontevedra · La Estrada · Lalín · Sarria · Villafranca del Bierzo · **LEÓN** · León · Saldaña · Osorno · Carrión Ferna
Ría Cangas-Marin · Chantada · Castro · Monforte · Ponferrada · El Teleno · 7,179 ▲ · Astorga · Valencia de Don Juan · Sahagún · Palencia · Condes · Astu
Vigo · Redondela · Carballino · Orense · Puebla de Trives · La Vega · La Bañeza · Villada · Fromista · Paredes de Nava · Villalón de Campos · Dueñas · Torq
Tuy · Túy · **ORENSE** · Allariz · Viana del Bollo · Benavente · Valderas · Medina de Rioseco · Valladolid · **VALLADOLID**
La Guardia · Minho · Celanova · Ginzo de Limia · Verín · Puebla de Sanabria · **ZAMORA** · Villalpando · Valladolid · Tudela de Duero · Cuéllar · Cantale
Caminha · Ponte-Arcos de Valdevez · Chaves · Vinhais · Bragança · Alcañices · Zamora · Toro · Medina del Campo · Olmedo · Iscar
Viana · **MINHO** · Braga · Fafe · Ribeira · **TRÁS-OS-MONTES** · Miranda do Douro · Bermillo de Sayago · Fuentesaúco · Nava del Rey · Rueda · Arévalo · **SEGOVIA** · Sar
Marinhas · Ofir · Barcelos · Guimarães · **E ALTO DOURO** · Mogadouro · Fermoselle · Ledesma · Madrigal · Peñaranda de Bracamonte · Segovia
Esposende · Póvoa de Varzim · Amarante · Vila Real · Alijó · Torre de Moncorvo · Vitigudino · **SALAMANCA** · Alba de Tormes · **ÁVILA**
Vila do Conde · Matosinhos · Orenfatel · Peso da Régua · Freixo · Nova de Fozcoa · Pinhel · Almeida · Salamanca · Peñaranda · Macotera · Ávila · Las Navas
Oporto (Porto) · Gondomar · Lamego · **DOURO** · da-Pesqueira · Ciudad Rodrigo · Fuentes de Oñoro · Guijuelo · Piedrahita · Cebreros · El Tiemblo
V. Nova de Gaia · **LITORAL** · Resende · Tarouca · Nova de · Trancoso · Vilar Formoso · Sequeros · Béjar · El Barco de Ávila · Almanzor · Gredos · 8,721 ▲ · Arenas de · San Martín
Vila da Feira · Castro Daire · Viseu · Celorico · Gouveia · **Guarda** · Fuentes de Oñoro · Hervás · Jarandilla · Candeleda · Fuensalida · Torrijos · Tole
Ílhavo · Aveiro · São João da Madeira · Mangualde · 6,532 ▲ · Hoyos · Sa. de Gata · Plasencia · Talavera · La Puebla · Oropesa · de la Reina · Tole
Vagos · Águeda · **BEIRA** · Nelas · Sabugal · Penamacor · Cilleros · Malpartida de Plasencia · Torrejoncillo · Navalmoral · Los Navalmorales · Mena
Cantanhede · Mira · C. Mondego · **ALTA** · Fundão · Monsanto · Coria · Plasencia · **S.** · Navalmoral de la Mata · Calzada · cillos · Montes de
Figueira da Foz · Montemor · Coimbra · Covilhã · Idanha · Mayor · Torrejoncillo · Navalvillar · Oropesa
Lavos · Miranda do Corvo · Góis · Castelo Branco · Rosmaninhal · Brozas · **CÁCERES** · Trujillo · Sa. de Guadalupe · Alía · Herrera · Ciudad Real
Louriçal · Soure · Lousã · **BEIRA** · Cáceres · Arroyo de la Luz · Casar de Cáceres · Logrosán · del Duque
Vieira de Leiria · Pombal · Oleiros · **BAIXA** · Valencia de Alcántara · S. Pedro · Miajadas · Orellana la Vieja · Puebla de Alcocer · Piedrabuena
Marinha Grande · Sertã · Vila Velha · Gálvez · Montánchez · Madroñera · Zorita · Madrigalejo · **CIUDAD**
Leiria · Batalha · Fátima · Tomar · Mação · Brozas · S. Pedro · Almoharín · Guareña · Villanueva de la Serena · Almadén · Almodóvar del Campo
S. Martinho do Porto · Porto de Mós · Abrantes · Gavião · Castelo de Vide · Campo Maior · Don Benito · Herrera del Duque · Puertollano
Nazaré · Caldas da Rainha · Rio Maior · Montargil · Alpalhão · **BADAJOZ** · Montijo · Quintana de la S. · Campanario · Almadén · Pozoblanco · Bañuelo · 4,547 ▲
Peniche · Óbidos · Cartaxo · Muge · Avis · Fronteira · Sousel · **Badajoz** · Villanueva de la Serena · Puebla de Alcocer · Villanueva de Córdoba · Andú
Torres Vedras · Santarém · Alpiarça · Alter do Chão · Arronches · Olivenza · Almendralejo · Zalamea · Hinojosa del Duque · Bélmez · Montoro
Lourinhã · Torres Novas · Coruche · Mora · Portalegre · Elvas · Barcarrota · Villafranca de los Barros · de la Serena · Fuente-Obejuna · **CÓRDOBA** · M
Ericeira · Mafra · Vila Franca de Xira · Vendas Novas · Estremoz · Jerez de los Caballeros · Llerena · Azuaga · Villanueva de Córdoba · Posadas
Sintra · Cascais · C. da Roca · Montijo · Alhos Vedros · Redondo · Fregenal de la Sierra · Los Santos de Maimona · Monasterio · **Sierra** · Córdoba · Porcu
LISBON · Baixa da Banheira · Montemor · Vila Viçosa · Reguengos · Jerez · Fuente de Cantos · Constantina · La Carlota · Bujalance · Carca
Estoril · Sesimbra · Setúbal · Évora · Mourão · Oliva · Aracena · Minas de Riotinto · Posadas · El Viso del · Montilla · Aguilar · Baena
C. Espichel · Alcácer do Sal · Vidigueira · Amareleja · Moura · Zalamea la Real · Nerva · Lora del Río · Carmona · Fuentes de Andalucía · Lucena · Priego
Bahia de Setúbal · Sado · Alvito · Ferreira do Alentejo · Beja · Barrancos · Valverde del Camino · El Arahal · Osuna · Rute · Monte
Grândola · Santiago do Cacém · **BAIXO** · Serpa · Aldea Nova · Aroche · **SEVILLE** · Alcalá · Marchena · Estepa · Campillos · Cordi
Alvalade · Sines · C. de Sines · **ALENTEJO** · Mértola · **HUELVA** · **Seville** · Utrera · Morón de la Frontera · Antequera · Colmenar
Vila Nova de Milfontes · Aljustrel · Castro Verde · Santa Olalla · Sanlúcar la Mayor · Montellano · **MÁLAGA** · **Málaga**
Odemira · Ourique · Almodóvar · Alcoutim · Zalamea la Real · Gibraleón · Las Marismas · Huelva · Arcos de la Frontera · Grazalema · Ronda · Coín · Alhaurín
S. Teotónio · Mira · Ayamonte · Moguer · Almonte · Coria · Utrera · Lebrija · Olvera · Marbella · Pta. de Cala Burras
Vila do Bispo · Sa. de Monchique · 2,959 ▲ · Castro Marim · Isla Cristina · Jerez · Estepona · Costa
C. St. Vincent · Lagos · Portimão · Silves · S. Brás · Olhão · Vila Real de Sto. Antonio · de la Frontera · Algeciras · La Línea · del Sol
ALGARVE · Loulé · Faro · C. de Sta. María · Sanlúcar de Barrameda · **CÁDIZ** · San Roque · **GIBRALTAR** (Br.) · Europa Pt.
Albufeira · Tavira · Gulf of · Cádiz · Rota · Pto. Real · El Puerto de Santa María · Ubrique · Jimena de la Frontera
Cádiz · San Fernando · Alcalá de los Gazules · Jimena · Tarifa · Strait of Gibraltar · Pta. de la Almiña
Chiclana de la Frontera · Medina Sidonia · C. de Trafalgar · Ceuta (Sp.)
Vejer de la Frontera · C. Spartel · **Tangier** · Tétouan · M

ATLANTIC OCEAN
MADEIRA
LITORAL
BEIRA
ESTREMADURA
RIBATEJO
ALTO ALENTEJO
BAIXO ALENTEJO

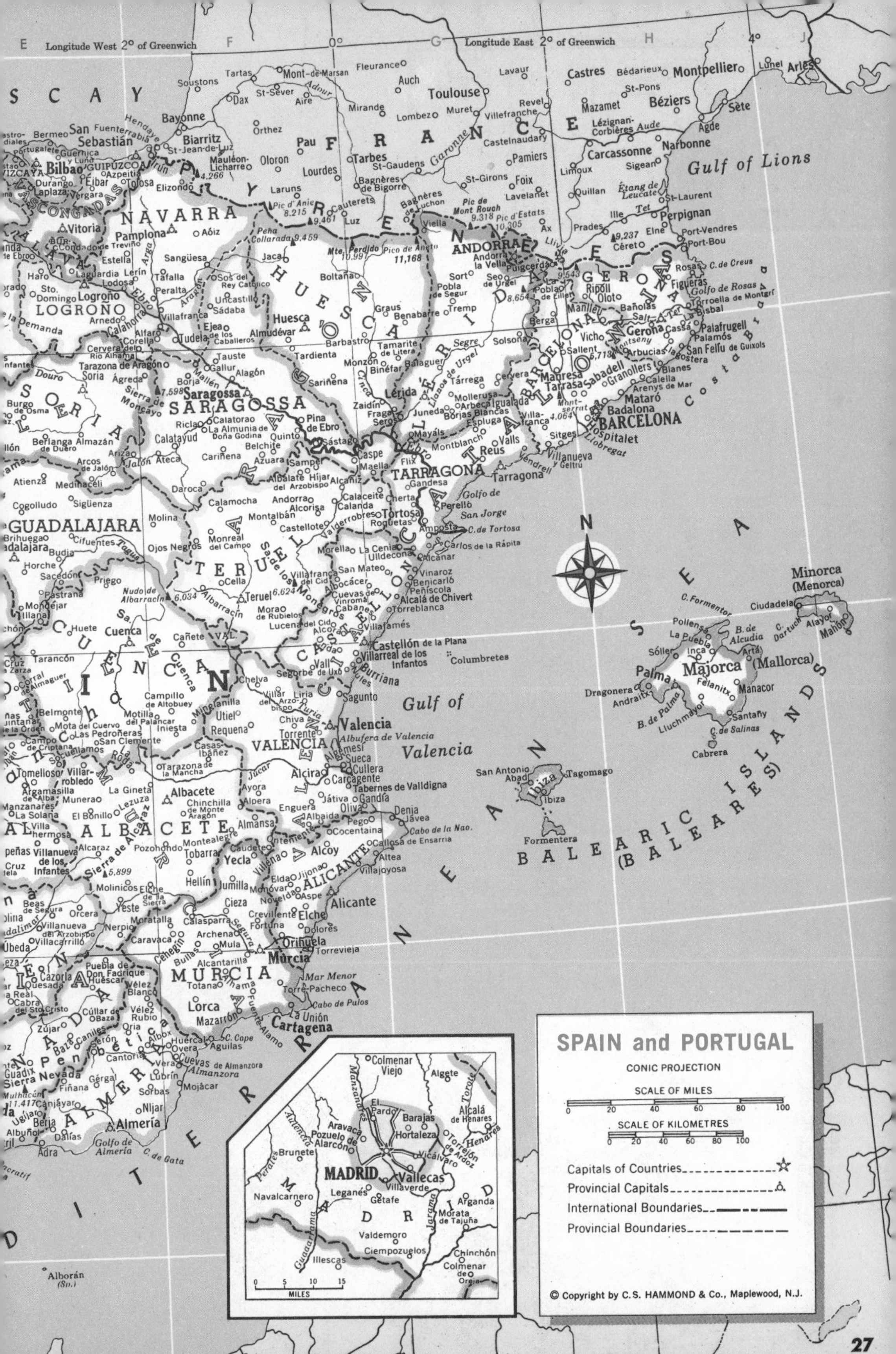
SPAIN and PORTUGAL
CONIC PROJECTION
SCALE OF MILES
0 20 40 60 80 100
SCALE OF KILOMETRES
0 20 40 60 80 100
Capitals of Countries
Provincial Capitals
International Boundaries
Provincial Boundaries
© Copyright by C.S. HAMMOND & Co., Maplewood, N.J.
Longitude West 2° of Greenwich
Longitude East 2° of Greenwich
FRANCE
PYRENEES
Gulf of Lions
MEDITERRANEAN SEA
BALEARIC ISLANDS (BALEARES)
Gulf of Valencia
NAVARRA
HUESCA
LERIDA
GERONA
BARCELONA
TARRAGONA
SARAGOSSA
TERUEL
CASTELLON
VALENCIA
ALICANTE
MURCIA
ALBACETE
CUENCA
GUADALAJARA
SORIA
LOGROÑO
ALMERIA
ANDORRA
Toulouse
Montpellier
Perpignan
Bayonne
Biarritz
San Sebastián
Bilbao
Vitoria
Pamplona
Logroño
Huesca
Lérida
Gerona
Barcelona
Tarragona
Saragossa
Teruel
Castellón de la Plana
Valencia
Alicante
Murcia
Cartagena
Albacete
Cuenca
Almería
Minorca (Menorca)
Majorca (Mallorca)
Ibiza
Formentera
Palma
Mahón
MADRID

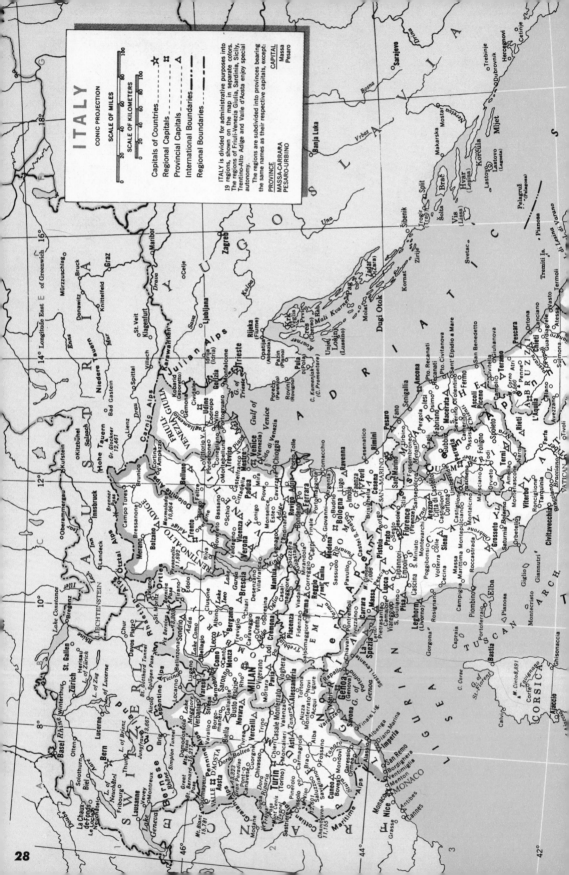

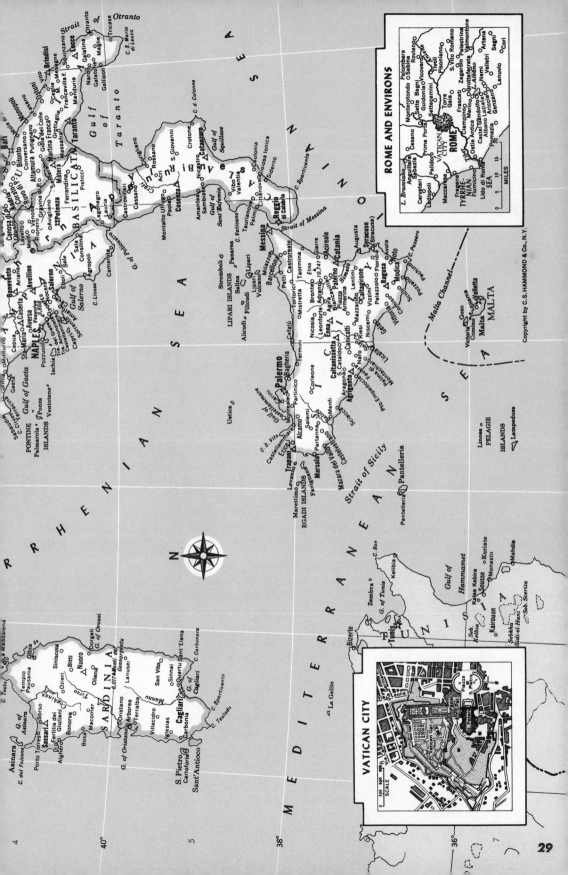

ROME AND ENVIRONS

L. Bracciano
Anguillara
Cerveteri
Ladispoli
Palidoro
Maccarese
Fregene
Lido di Roma
TYRRHE-
NIAN
SEA
Fiumicino
Ostia Antica
Castel Fusano
Ostia Lido
Albano Laziale
VATICAN
CITY
ROME
Palombara
Montorotondo
Cesano
Sabazia
Prima Porta
Settecamini
Torre
Gaia
Ciampino
Frascati
Marino
Castel Gandolfo
Grottaferrata
Monterotondo
Sabina
Roviano
S. Vito Romano
Guidonia
Vicovaro
Tivoli
Zagarolo
Palestrina
Valmontone
L. Albano
Nemi
Genzano
Velletri
Artena
Segni
Cori
Lanuvio

MILES
0   5   10   15

VATICAN CITY

SCALE
FEET
0 100 300 600

Piazza
S. Pietro
Vatican Gar.
Leone

Gozo
Victoria
Comino
Malta
MALTA
Gozo
Marsa
Valletta
Cittavecchia

Malta Channel

PELAGIE
ISLANDS
Linosa
Lampedusa

TUNISIA
Bizerte
Tunis
Zembra
G. of Tunis
C. Bon
Kelibia
Gulf of
Hammamet
Kalaa Kebira
Sousse
Monastir
Kairouan
Seb.
Kelbia
Seb.
Sidi-el-Hani
Seb. Scerita
Mahdia
Kuriate
La Galite

Brindisi
Lecce
Strait of Otranto
Tricase
Otranto
BASILICATA
Gulf of Taranto
Taranto
CALABRIA
Catanzaro
Gulf of Squillace
Crotone
Cosenza
Reggio di Calabria
Strait of Messina
Messina
Etna 10,741
Catania
Syracuse (Siracusa)
Palermo
Marsala
Trapani
Strait of Sicily
Pantelleria

NAPLES
Gulf of Salerno
Salerno
Benevento
Avellino
Caserta
Gulf of Gaeta
PONTINE ISLANDS
Palmarola
Ventotene

TYRRHENIAN SEA

MEDITERRANEAN SEA

SARDINIA
Cagliari
Nuoro
Sassari
Oristano
Monti del Gennargentu 6,017
G. of Cagliari
G. of Oristano
G. of Asinara
Asinara
S. Pietro
Sant'Antioco
C. Spartivento
C. Teulada

N

29

33

THE
BALKAN STATES

CONIC PROJECTION

SCALE OF MILES
0   25   50   75   100   125   150   175

SCALE OF KILOMETRES
0 25 50 75 100 125 150 175

Capitals of Countries .... ✪

Administrative Centers .... △

International Boundaries ----------

Major Internal Boundaries --------

Minor Internal Boundaries --------

Canals ....

BULGARIA and GREECE are divided into counties and departments, respectively. Because of the scale no attempt has been made to delimit and name these sub-divisions; their administrative centers have, however, been designated.

The larger divisions named in Greece are well-known geographical regions, without administrative function.

RUMANIA consists of sixteen regions and two in-dependent administrative units, Bucharest City and Constanţa Town.

ALBANIA is divided into prefectures, bearing the same names as their administrative centers.

YUGOSLAVIA is a federation of six republics. The Serbian republic includes an autonomous province (Voyvodina), and an autonomous region (Kosovo-Mitohyan).

UNION OF SOVIET SOCIALIST REPUBLICS
European Part

CONIC PROJECTION

SCALE OF MILES
0   50   100   200   300

SCALE OF KILOMETRES
0 50 100   200   300

National Capitals	☆
Capitals of Union Republics	⊠
Administrative Centers	△
International boundaries	
Union Republic boundaries	
A.S.S.R., Oblast, Kray boundaries	
Autonomous Oblast boundaries	
National Okrug boundaries	
Canals	

The government of the United States has not recognized the incorporation of Estonia, Latvia and Lithuania into the Soviet Union, nor does it recognize as final the de facto western limit of Polish administration in Germany (the Oder-Neisse line).

36

Administrative Divisions bear same
names as their respective Capitals
or Centers, except:

Abkhaz A.S.S.R.	F6	Sukhumi	F6	
Adgey Aut. Oblast	F6	Maykop	F6	
Adzhar A.S.S.R.	F6	Batumi	J4	
Bashkir A.S.S.R.	G6	Ufa	G6	
Chechen-Ingush A.S.S.R.	G3	Groznyy	G3	
Chuvash A.S.S.R.	G3	Cheboksary	D6	
Crimen Oblast	D6	Simferopol'	G6	
Dagestan A.S.S.R.	G6	Makhachkala	F5	
Kabardin-Balkar A.S.S.R.	F5	Nal'chik		
Kalmuck A.S.S.R.	F6	Elista		
Karachay-Cherkess Aut. Obl.	F6	Cherkessk	F6	
Karelian A.S.S.R.	D2	Petrozavodsk	D2	
Komi A.S.S.R.	H2	Syktyvkar	H2	
Komi-Permyak Nat'l Okrug	H3	Kudymkar	H3	
Mari A.S.S.R.	G3	Yoshkar-Ola	G3	
Mordvinian A.S.S.R.	G4	Saransk	G4	
Nagorno-Karabakh Aut. Obl.	G7	Stepanakert	G7	
Nenets Nat'l Okrug	H1	Nar'yan-Mar	H1	
North Ossetian A.S.S.R.	F6	Ordzhonikidze	F6	
South Ossetian Aut. Obl.	G3	Tskhinvali	G3	
Tatar A.S.S.R.	B5	Kazan'	B5	
Trans-Carpathian Oblast	H3	Uzhgorod	H3	
Udmurt A.S.S.R.	C4	Izhevsk	C4	
Volyn Oblast		Lutsk		

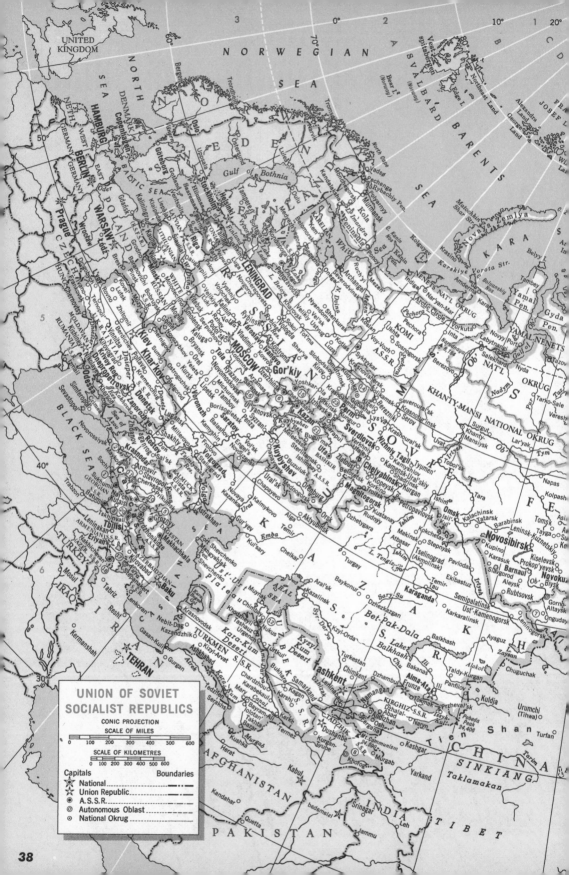

UNION OF SOVIET
SOCIALIST REPUBLICS

CONIC PROJECTION
SCALE OF MILES
0 100 200 300 400 500 600

SCALE OF KILOMETRES
0 100 200 300 400 500 600

Capitals   Boundaries
⊛ National ....
☆ Union Republic ....
⊚ A.S.S.R. ....
⊚ Autonomous Oblast ....
⊙ National Okrug ....

38

REPUBLIC OF THE PHILIPPINES

Luzon
Quezon City
Manila
Mindanao

Moluccas
CELEBES SEA
Celebes
BANDA SEA
Flores
Timor
Sumbawa
Sumba
Bali
Java
JAVA SEA

AUSTRALIA

BRUNEI (British)
Sabah
Borneo
SARAWAK
MALAYSIA
SINGAPORE
Medan
Djakarta
Sumatra
INDONESIA

HONG KONG (British)
Canton
Hainan
NORTH VIET-NAM
Hanoi
SOUTH VIETNAM
CAMBODIA
Saigon
China
SOUTH CHINA SEA
Kunming
Mekong R.
Salween River
THAILAND
Bangkok
Gulf of Siam
Phnom Penh

BURMA
Rangoon
Irrawaddy River
ANDAMAN SEA
Andaman Is. (Indian)
Nicobar Is. (Indian)

PAK
Katmandu
Mt. Ganges
Calcutta
INDIA
Hyderabad
DECCAN PLATEAU
Madras
Bombay
Ahmadabad
New Delhi
Karachi
Tropic of Cancer

BAY OF BENGAL

CEYLON
Dondra Head
Cape Comorin
Colombo
Equator

Laccadive Is. (Indian)
MALDIVE ISLANDS

ARABIAN SEA

BRITISH INDIAN OCEAN TERR.

INDIAN OCEAN

Tropic of Capricorn

Seychelles (British)

MAURITIUS

Réunion (French)

Madagascar
MALAGASY REP.

OMAN
TRUCIAL OMAN
Rub' al Khali Desert
MUSCAT
Socotra (So. Yemen)
Gulf of Aden
SOUTHERN YEMEN
Madinat ash Sha'b
YEMEN
San'a
Taizz
ETHIOPIA
SOMALI REP.
ARABIA

Map of ASIA

SCALE OF MILES

0   200   400   600   800   1000

Capitals of Countries ●
Cities ●
Boundaries of Countries
Other Boundaries
Mountain Peaks ▲
Canals

Water
Lowlands
Depression
Highlands
Mountains

Copyright by C. S. Hammond & Co., N.Y.

20°   30°   40°

Greenwich   120°

East of   110°

Longitude   100°

90°

80°

70°

60°

50°

40°

30°

20°

10°

0°

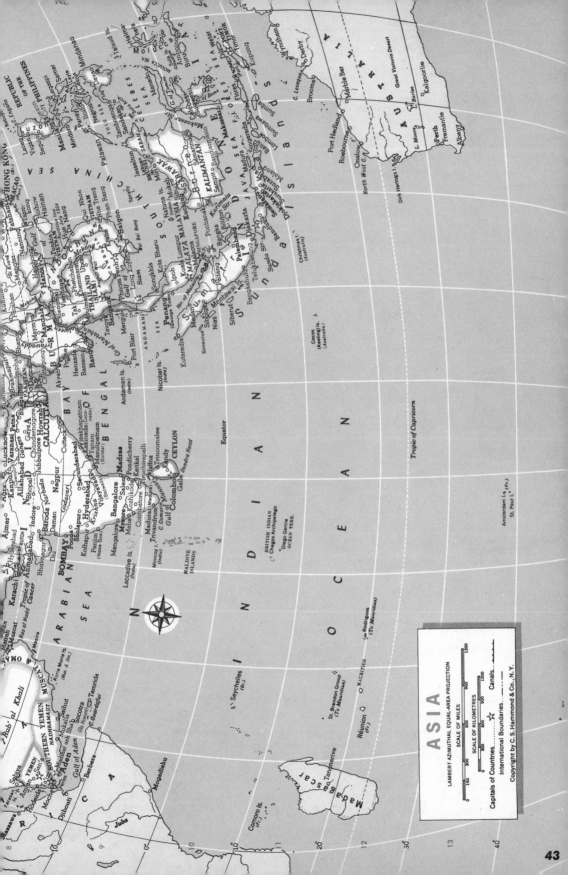

ASIA
LAMBERT AZIMUTHAL EQUAL-AREA PROJECTION

SCALE OF MILES
0   150   300   450   600   750   900   1200

SCALE OF KILOMETRES
0   300   600   900   1200

Capitals of Countries .... ☆
International Boundaries ....
Canals ....

Copyright by C. S. Hammond & Co., N.Y.

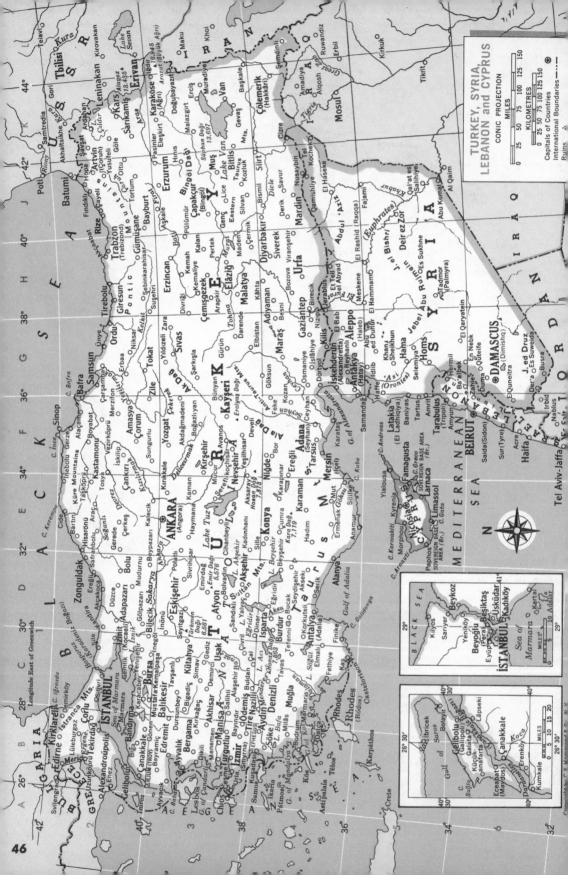

ISRAEL and JORDAN

CYLINDRICAL PROJECTION

Copyright by C.S. HAMMOND & CO., N.Y.

SCALE OF MILES

0 5 10 15 20 25 30

SCALE OF KILOMETRES

0 5 10 15 20 25 30

Capitals of Countries .... ☆
District and Provincial Capitals .... ⊙
International Boundaries .... —·—·—
District and Provincial Boundaries ...... ———
Demilitarized Zone Boundaries ....
Neutral Zone Boundaries ....

47

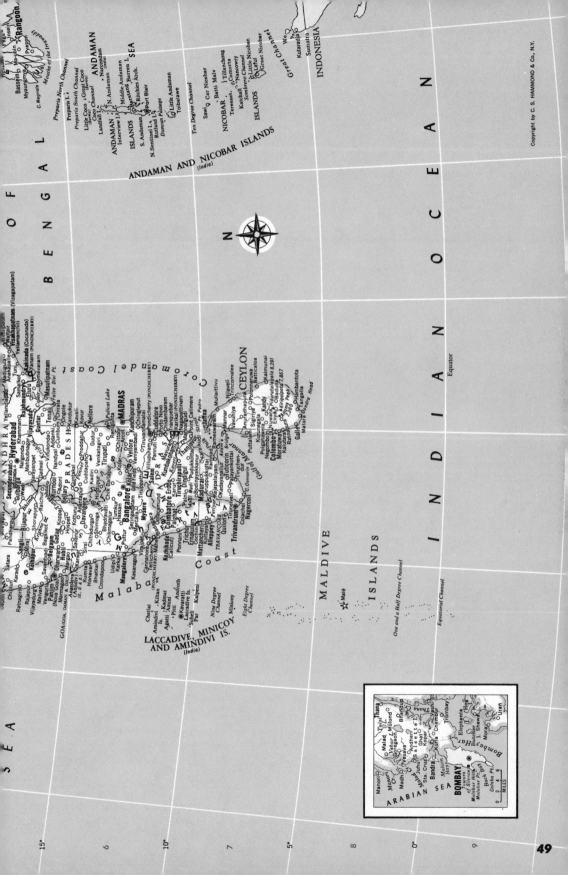

This is a map of India (southern portion), Ceylon, and the surrounding region, with the following notable labels:

BAY OF BENGAL

ANDAMAN SEA

ANDAMAN ISLANDS
- N. Andaman
- Middle Andaman
- S. Andaman
- Port Blair
- Little Andaman
- Ritchie Arch.
- Rutland Passage
- Duncan Passage
- Interview I.
- Landfall I.
- Barren I. (India)
- Narcondam
- N. Sentinel I.

NICOBAR ISLANDS
- Car Nicobar
- Batti Malv
- Tillanchong
- Camorta
- Nancowry
- Teressa
- Katchall
- Sombrero Channel
- Little Nicobar
- Laful
- Great Nicobar

ANDAMAN AND NICOBAR ISLANDS (India)

INDONESIA
- Kutaradja
- Sumatra
- We

ANDHRA PRADESH
- Hyderabad
- Secunderabad
- Visakhapatnam (Vizagapatam)

MADRAS

MYSORE
- Bangalore
- Mysore

KERALA

CEYLON
- Colombo
- Kandy
- Trincomalee
- Jaffna
- Galle

INDIAN OCEAN

Equator

MALDIVE ISLANDS
- Malé
- One and a Half Degree Channel
- Equatorial Channel
- Eight Degree Channel
- Nine Degree Channel

LACCADIVE, MINICOY AND AMINDIVI IS. (India)

Malabar Coast

Coromandel Coast

ARABIAN SEA

Inset map: **BOMBAY** (Bombay Harbour)
- Thana
- Bandra
- Elephanta
- Trombay
- Uran

Copyright by C. S. HAMMOND & Co., N.Y.

49

CHINA and MONGOLIA

CONIC PROJECTION

SCALE OF MILES

0   100   200   300   400   500

SCALE OF KILOMETRES

0   100   200   300   400   500

Capitals of Countries....★   International Boundaries..._.._

Provincial Capitals........◉   Provincial Boundaries....._.._

Canals ....++++++   Walls ....ᴧᴧᴧᴧᴧᴧ

Copyright by C. S. Hammond & Co., N. Y.

*Wuhan municipality consists of
Hankow, Hanyang and Wuchang
†Lüta municipality includes
Port Arthur and Dairen

51

TOKYO

KYUSHU

PACIFIC OCEAN

HOKKAIDO

HONSHU

RYUKYU ISLANDS

SAKISHIMA ISLANDS

Tropic of Cancer

KYOTO · OSAKA · KOBE

SEA OF JAPAN

U.S.S.R.

Lake Khanka

Vladivostok

NORTH KOREA

SOUTH KOREA

Seoul

P'yŏngyang

MANCHURIA

CHINA

SHIKOKU

KYUSHU

PACIFIC OCEAN

YELLOW SEA

EAST CHINA SEA

Cheju (Quelpart)

52

BURMA, THAILAND, INDOCHINA and MALAYA

CONIC PROJECTION

SCALE OF MILES
0 50 100   200   300

SCALE OF KILOMETRES
0 50 100   200   300

Capitals of Countries .... ⊛
Capitals of States .... ⊙
International Boundaries ....

INDEX MAP — SOUTHEAST ASIA / JAVA

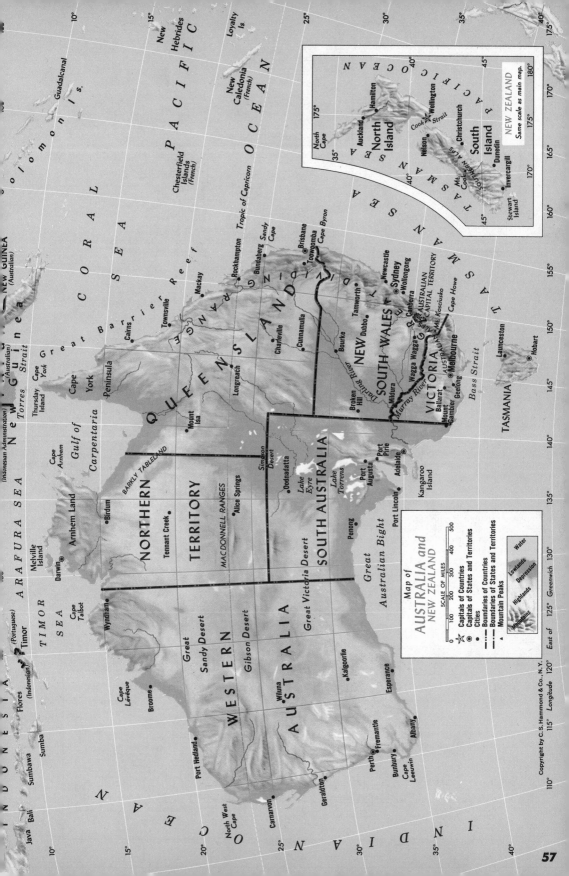

Map of AUSTRALIA and NEW ZEALAND

⊙ Capitals of Countries
⊛ Capitals of States and Territories
• Cities
···· Boundaries of Countries
▬▬ Boundaries of States and Territories
▲ Mountain Peaks

SCALE OF MILES
0 100 200 300 400 500

Water
Lowlands
Depression
Highlands
Mountains

Copyright by C.S. Hammond & Co., N.Y.

NEW ZEALAND
Same scale as main map.

North Cape
Auckland
Hamilton
North Island
TASMAN SEA
Cook Strait
Nelson
Wellington
PACIFIC OCEAN
Christchurch
Mt. Cook
SOUTHERN ALPS
South Island
Dunedin
Invercargill
Stewart Island

PACIFIC OCEAN

New Hebrides
Loyalty Is.
New Caledonia (French)
Guadalcanal
Solomon Is.
Chesterfield Islands (French)

CORAL SEA
Great Barrier Reef
Tropic of Capricorn

NEW GUINEA (Australian)
(Indonesian Administration)
NEW GUINEA
Torres Strait
Thursday Island
Cape York
Cape York Peninsula
Gulf of Carpentaria

ARAFURA SEA
TIMOR SEA
Cape Arnhem
Arnhem Land
Melville Island
Cape Talbot
Darwin
Cape Lévêque
Broome

Timor (Portuguese)
Flores (Indonesian)
Sumba
Sumbawa
Bali
Java
INDONESIA

Birdum
Tennant Creek
Barkly Tableland

NORTHERN TERRITORY
Alice Springs
MACDONNELL RANGES
Mount Isa

QUEENSLAND
Townsville
Cairns
Mackay
Rockhampton
Longreach
Charleville
Cunnamulla
Bundaberg
Sandy Cape
Brisbane
Toowoomba
Cape Byron

GREAT DIVIDING RANGE

WESTERN AUSTRALIA
Great Sandy Desert
Gibson Desert
Great Victoria Desert
Wiluna
Kalgoorlie
Esperance
Perth
Fremantle
Bunbury
Albany
Cape Leeuwin
Geraldton
Carnarvon
North West Cape
Port Hedland

Simpson Desert
Oodnadatta
Lake Eyre
SOUTH AUSTRALIA
Lake Torrens
Penong
Port Augusta
Port Pirie
Port Lincoln
Adelaide
Kangaroo Island
Great Australian Bight

NEW SOUTH WALES
Broken Hill
Bourke
Dubbo
Tamworth
Newcastle
Sydney
Wollongong
Darling River
Wagga Wagga
Mildura
AUSTRALIAN CAPITAL TERRITORY
Canberra
Mt. Kosciusko
Cape Howe

VICTORIA
Murray River
Ballarat
Melbourne
Geelong
Mount Gambier
Bass Strait

TASMANIA
Launceston
Hobart

INDIAN OCEAN
TASMAN SEA

57

AUSTRALIA and NEW ZEALAND

BONNE PROJECTION

SCALE OF MILES

0   50   100   200   300   400   500

SCALE OF KILOMETRES

0   50   100   200   300   400   500

Capital of Country ... ☆   State and Territorial Capitals ... △

59

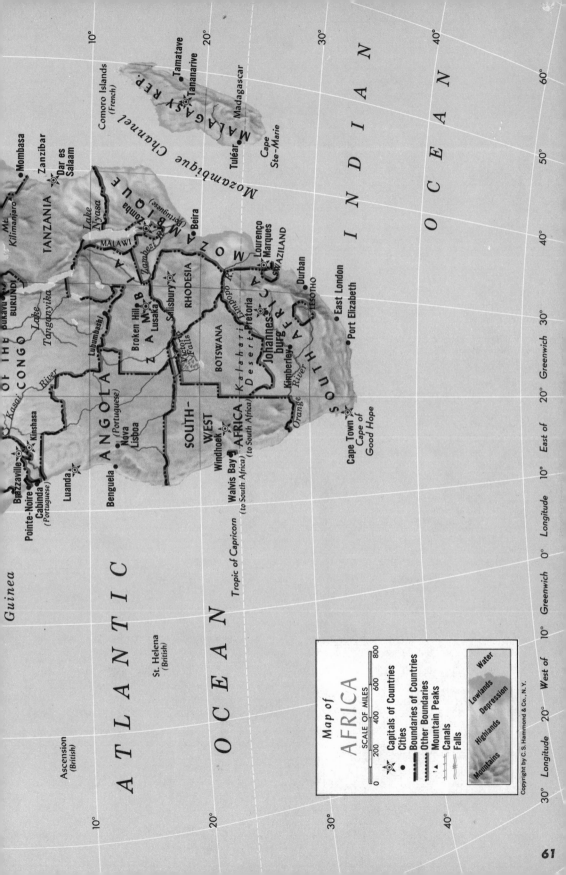

Map of

AFRICA

SCALE OF MILES

0   200   400   600   800

* Capitals of Countries
• Cities
━━ Boundaries of Countries
••••• Other Boundaries
▲ Mountain Peaks
Canals
Falls

Water
Lowlands
Depression
Highlands
Mountains

Guinea

ATLANTIC

OCEAN

Ascension
(British)

St. Helena
(British)

Tropic of Capricorn

Longitude   West of   Greenwich   Longitude   0°   East of   Greenwich

10°   20°   30°   40°   10°   0°   10°   20°   30°

Brazzaville
Pointe-Noire
Cabinda
(Portuguese)
Kinshasa
Luanda

Benguela
Nova
Lisboa

ANGOLA
(Portuguese)

CONGO
Kasai River
Kasai

OF THE

BURUNDI
Lake
Tanganyika
Bukavu

Lubumbashi

Broken Hill
ZAMBIA
Lusaka
Victoria
Falls

Windhoek

Walvis Bay
(to South Africa)

SOUTH-WEST AFRICA
(to South Africa)

BOTSWANA

Kalahari Desert

Orange River
Orange

Kimberley

Johannes-
burg
Pretoria
SOUTH AFRICA

Limpopo R.

Sallsbury
RHODESIA

Zambezi

MALAWI
Lake
Nyasa
Zomba

Beira

MOZAMBIQUE
(Portuguese)

Lourenço
Marques
SWAZILAND

Durban
LESOTHO
East London
Port Elizabeth

Cape Town
Cape of
Good Hope

TANZANIA
Mt.
Kilimanjaro
Mombasa
Zanzibar
Dar es
Salaam

Mozambique Channel

Comoro Islands
(French)

Tamatave
Tananarive

Madagascar

MALAGASY REP.

Tuléar
Cape
Ste-Marie

INDIAN

OCEAN

10°   20°   30°   40°

10°   20°   30°   40°   50°   60°

This is a map of Northwest Africa and Western Europe.

Compass directions and grid references:
30° A 25° B 20° C 15° D E 10° E 5° F 0° G 5° H 10°

IRELAND
UNITED KINGDOM
NORTH SEA
London
Hamburg
GERMANY
Bonn
LUX.
BELGIUM
NETH.
Prag
English Channel
Paris
Seine
Danube
FRANCE
SWITZ.
AUST
Bay of Biscay
Loire
Rhône
Marseille
Corsica
ANDORRA
Rome
Madrid
Barcelona
Sardinia
Naples
SPAIN
TYRRHENIA
SEA
PORTUGAL
Lisbon
Tagus
Balearic Is.
Guadalquivir
Douro
Ebro

NORTH

ATLANTIC

OCEAN

Ponta Delgada
São Miguel
Sta. Cruz
AZORES
(Port.)

Madeira
(Port.)
Funchal
Pôrto Santo
Desertas

CANARY ISLANDS
(Sp.)
La Palma
Gomera
Hierro
Sta. Cruz
Tenerife
Grand Canary
Las Palmas
Fuerteventura
Lanzarote
Salvage Is. (Port.)

Tropic of Cancer

GIBRALTAR (Br.)
Str. of Gibraltar
Tangier
Ceuta (Sp.)
Tetuan (Sp.)
Larache
Ouezzano
Kénitra (Port-Lyautey)
Rabat
Casablanca
Azemmour
El Jadida (Mazagan)
Safi
C. Cantin
Essaouira (Mogador)
Marrakech
Taroudant
Tiznit
IFNI (Sp.)
Sidi Ifni
Agadir
C. Sim
Settat
Meknès
Fez
Khenifra
Figuig
Taza
Oujda

MOROCCO

Oran (El Dzejari)
Algiers (El Djezair)
Mostaganem
Blida
Tlemcen
Saïda
Mascara
Tiaret
Tizi-Ouzou
Bougie
Bouira
Setif
Constantine
Skikda
Bône
Tébessa
Annaba
Tunis
Bizerte
G. of Tunis
C. Bon
G. of Hammamet
Sousse
Moknine
Kairouan
Sfax
Kerkennah Is.
G. of Gabès
Djerba
Gabès
Médenine
Zarzis
Tripoli
Aziziia
Gharian
Nalut
Beni Ulid
Mizda
Sinawen
Derj
Ghadames

ALGERIA

SPANISH SAHARA

Villa Cisneros
Bir Nzaran
Bir Moghrein (Ft-Trinquet)
Tindouf
Semara
el Hamra
Saguia
El Aaiún
C. Bojador
C. Blanco
Port-Étienne
C. Barbas
Ganduz
Lévrier Bay
C. Timiris
Nouakchott
Akreidil
Méderdra
Rosso
Boghe
St-Louis
Louga
Thiès
Rufisque
Dakar
C. Verde
Bathurst
GAMBIA
Ziguinchor

MAURITANIA

TRIPO
FEZZ

SAHARA

SENEGAL

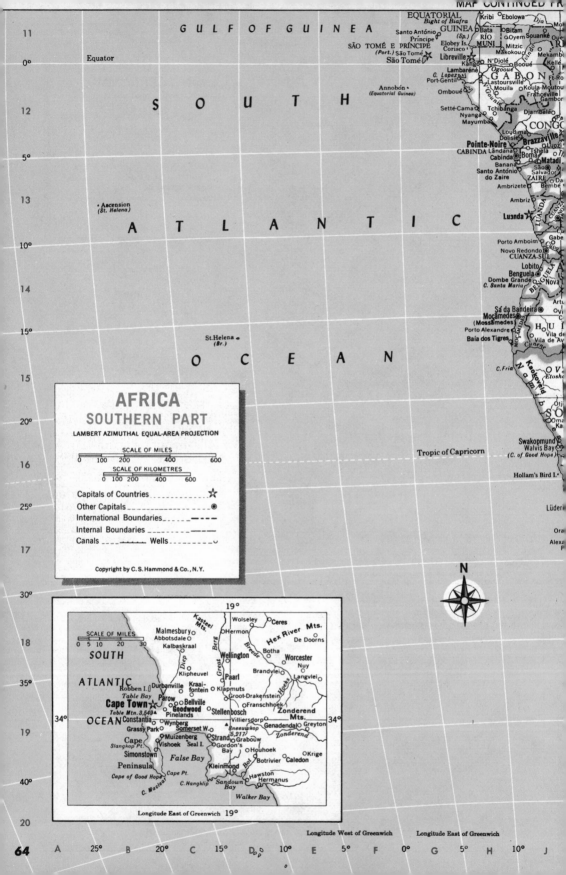

AFRICA
SOUTHERN PART
LAMBERT AZIMUTHAL EQUAL-AREA PROJECTION

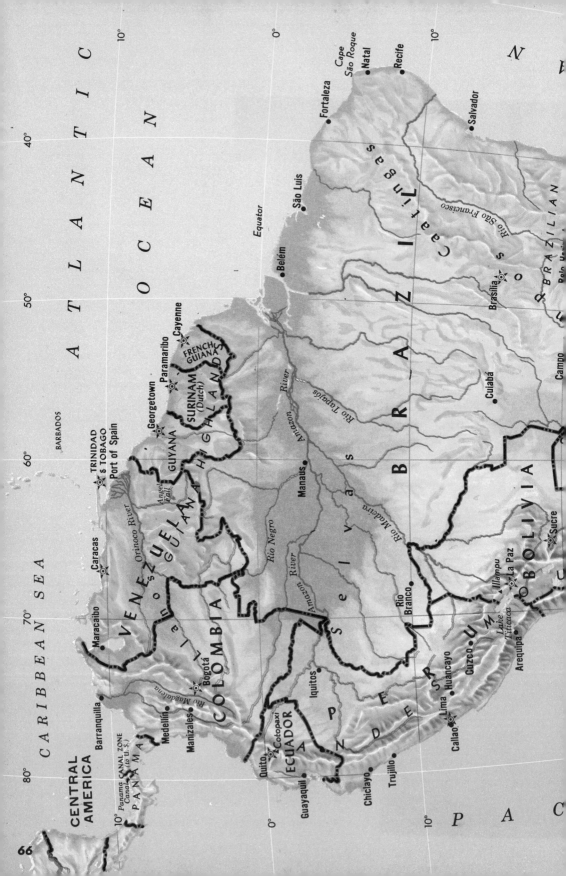

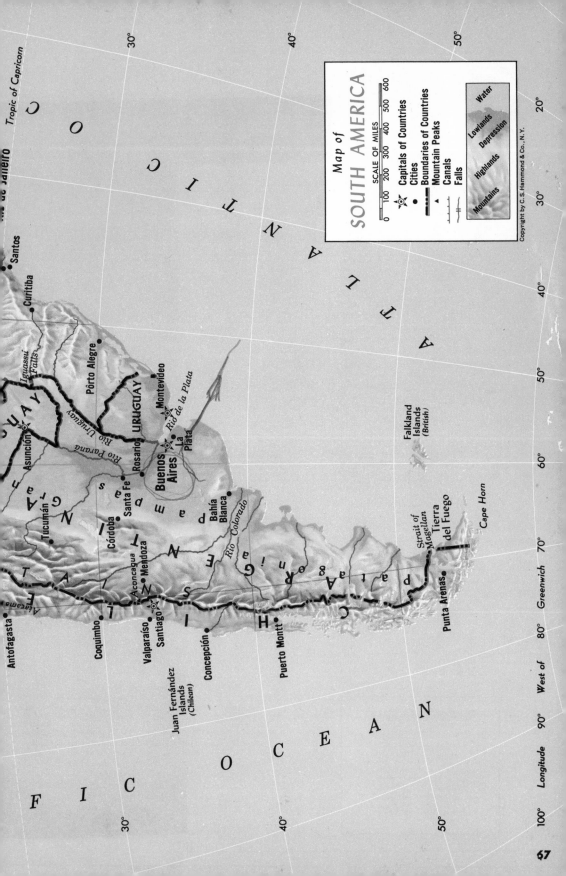

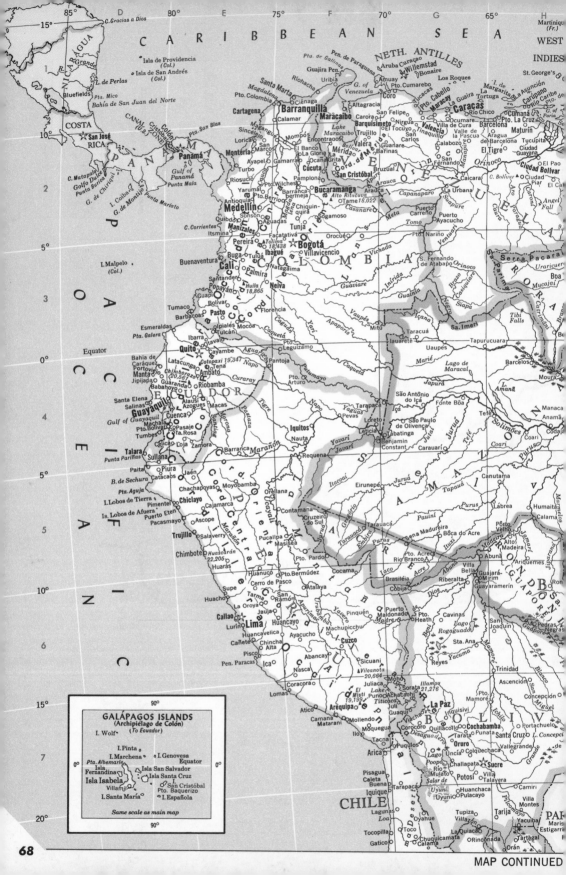

SOUTH AMERICA
NORTHERN PART
LAMBERT AZIMUTHAL EQUAL-AREA PROJECTION

SCALE OF MILES
0 100 200 300 400 500

SCALE OF KILOMETRES
0 100 200 300 400 500

Capitals of Countries............☆
Other Capitals ....△
International Boundaries......—·—
Other Boundaries...........—··—

Copyright by C.S. Hammond & Co., N.Y.

ATLANTIC OCEAN

Equator

SURINAM
FRENCH
GUIANA
(Neth.)

Georgetown
Paramaribo
Cayenne

AMAPÁ
Macapá

P A R Á

Amazonas

Belém
Marajó

Santarém

M A R A N H Ã O

Fortaleza
(Ceará)

Teresina

Parnaíba

São Luís

RIO GRANDE
DO NORTE
Natal

C E A R Á

P I A U Í

Juàzeiro
do Norte

PARAÍBA
Campina Grande
João Pessoa
(Paraíba)
Olinda
Caruaru
Recife
(Pernambuco)

PERNAMBUCO

ALAGOAS
Maceió

SERGIPE
Aracaju

B R A Z I L

G O I Á S

B A H I A

Feira de Santana

Salvador (Bahia)

Jequié

Vitória da
Conquista

Ilhéus

MATO GROSSO

Cuiabá

Campo
Grande

Goiânia

DISTRITO
FEDERAL

Brasília

M I N A S

G E R A I S

Belo
Horizonte

Uberlândia

Juiz
de Fora

ESPÍRITO
SANTO

Vitória

SÃO PAULO

Ribeirão
Prêto

Bauru

RIO DE JANEIRO

C. de São Tomé

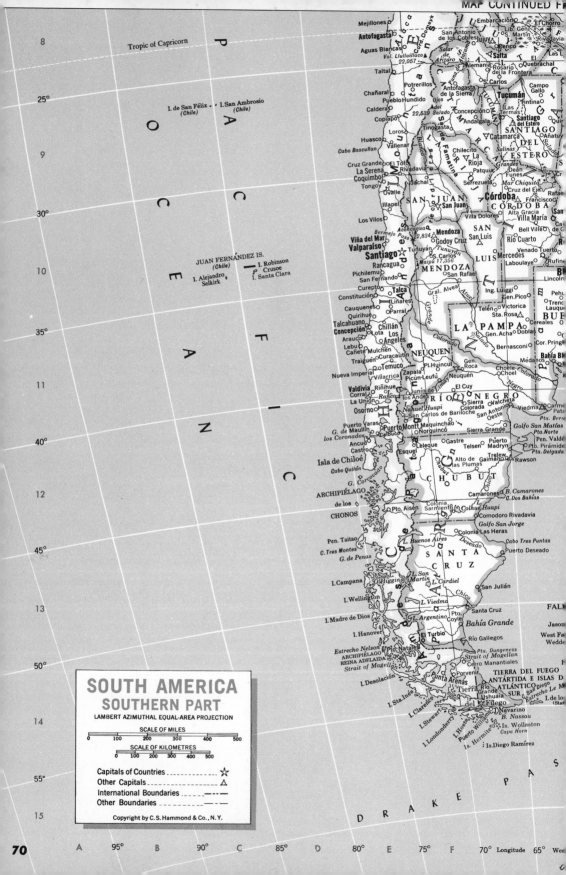

Tropic of Capricorn

BRAZIL

PARANÁ

SÃO PAULO
RIO DE JANEIRO

Niterói
Petrópolis
Volta Redonda
Campinas
Botucatu
Sorocaba
S. Bernardo do Campo
Jundiaí
Santos
Curitiba
Ponta Grossa
Paranaguá
Castro
Iguape
Guarapuava
Foz do Iguaçu
Iguassú Falls
União da Vitória
São Francisco do Sul
SANTA CATARINA
Blumenau
Itajaí
Joinville
Florianópolis
I. de Sta. Catarina
Lajes
Tubarão
Araranguá
Caxias do Sul
S. Leopoldo
RIO GRANDE DO SUL
Pôrto Alegre
Passo Fundo
Erechim
Sto. Angelo
Ijuí
Cruz Alta
Veranópolis
Cachoeira do Sul
Rio Pardo
Santa Maria
Pelotas
Rio Grande
Lagôa dos Patos
Laguna Mirim
Lagôa da Mangueira
Santa Vitória do Palmar

PARAGUAY
Amambaí
Horqueta
San Pedro
Villa
Concepción
Bernardino
Luque
Villarrica
Caazapá
Encarnación
Posadas
Corrientes
Empedrado
Paso de los Libres
Uruguaiana
Alegrete
Artigas
Bella Unión
Salto
Paysandú
Tacuarembó
Bagé
Melo

URUGUAY
Paso de los Toros
Durazno
Trinidad
Florida
Minas
San José
Canelones
Rocha
MONTEVIDEO
Maldonado

La Plata
Río de la Plata
C. San Antonio
Gen. Juan Madariaga
Mar del Plata
Gen. Alvarado (Miramar)

SOUTH ORKNEY IS.
Coronation I.
Laurie I.

Elephant I.
Clarence I.
East Falkland
Stanley
Choiseul Sd.

Santiago Inset

MILES 0 15 30

Petorca
Papudo
La Ligua
Putaendo
Quintero
La Calera
Llay-Llay
San Felipe
Los Andes
Aconcagua 22,834
ARGENTINA
Viña del Mar
Pta. Curaumilla
Quillota
Limache
VALPARAÍSO
SANTIAGO
Algarrobo
Cartagena
Curacaví
Melipilla
San Antonio
Pta. Toro
San Bernardo
Paine
El Volcán
Pta. Topocalma
Las Cabras
Rancagua
El Teniente
Sewell
Maipú 17,356
Pichilemu
Peumo
San Fernando
Santa Cruz

PACIFIC OCEAN
72° 70° 34°

Buenos Aires Inset

Acevedo
San Pedro
ENTRE RÍOS
Agraciada
Nueva Palmira
URUGUAY
Colón
Pergamino
Baradero
Sta. Lucía
Carabelas
Arrecifes
V. Lía
Lima
Zárate
Carmelo
Joaquín Suárez
M. García (Arg.)
Rojas
S. Antonio de Areco
Campana
Capilla del Señor
Colonia
Salto
Carmen de Areco
C'nl. Isleño
BUENOS
San Fernando
San Isidro
Tigre
BUENOS AIRES
Junín
Chacabuco
S. Andrés de Giles
Rivas
Luján
DIST. FED.
Avellaneda
Morón
Lanús
Quilmes
Emilio Ayarza
Suipacha
Mercedes
Ensenada
Irala
Alberti
Chivilcoy
AIRES
Marcos Paz
Lomas de Zamora
Adrogué
La Plata
Magdalena
G'ral. O'Brien
Los Toldos
Navarro
Gral. Las Heras
Cañuelas
San Vicente
C'nl. Brandsen
Bragado
Norberto de la Riestra
Lobos
Roque Pérez
SCALE OF MILES 0 20 40 60
60° 58°

Rio de Janeiro Inset

43° 20' 43° 10'
SCALE OF MILES 0 2 4 6

Baía de Guanabara
RIO DE JANEIRO
Duque de Caxias
Ilha do Boqueirão
Pta. do Tubiaçanga
I. de Paquetá
São João de Meriti
S. João de Meriti
Pavuna
Saravatá
Ilha do Governador
Freguezia
Cocotá
Ilha dos Tavares
Anchieta
Vigário Geral
Ilha do Engenho
Ricardo de Albuquerque
Colégio
Irajá
Olaria
Pta. do Galeão
I. do Fundão
Baía de
Neves
Vila Nova
Deodoro
Penha
Ramos
I. do Bom Jesus
I. da Sapucaia
Guanabara
Niterói
Icaraí
Vila Militar
Madureira
Inhaúma
Méier
Eng. Novo
Aeropôrto S. Dumont
RIO DE JANEIRO
Bangú
Realengo
Piedade
Andaraí
Tijuca
Rio Comprido
Glória
Sa. do Barata
Sa. do Engenho Velho
Rio Grande
Jacarepaguá
Pico da Tijuca 3,350
Corcovado 2,310
Botafogo
Sugar Loaf 1,296
Pedra Branca 3,370
Morro da Taquara
L. Rodrigo de Freitas
Alto da Bôa Vista
Copacabana
Vargem Pequena
GUANABARA
I. de Jacarepaguá
Gávea
Leblon
Ipanema
Pta. do Arpoador
I. da Pae
Lagôa Marapendi
Lagôa Tijuca
Pta. do Marisco
Ilha das Palmas
Ilha Cagarra
Ilha de Meio
Ilha Pontuda
I. da Alfavaca
Ilha Comprida
ATLANTIC
43° 20' 43° 10'
22° 50' 23°

OCEAN
ATLANTIC

CANADA

Bermuda
(British)

Tropic of Cancer

PUERTO
RICO
(to U.S.)

Bahama Islands
(British)

DOMINICAN
REPUBLIC

HAITI

WEST INDIES

Cape Kennedy

Jacksonville

Miami

Atlanta

Mt. Mitchell

APPAL.

Memphis

New Orleans

Mississippi River

Dallas

Houston

Houston

Rio Grande

El Paso

Monterrey

Guadalajara

Mt. Whitney

Mexico City

Veracruz

Mt. Logan Colony

Phoenix

Los Angeles

San Diego

NEVADA

Lower California

Gulf of Mexico

CUBA

Havana

JAMAICA

Yucatán
Peninsula

BRITISH
HONDURAS

GUATEMALA

EL SALVADOR

HONDURAS

NICARAGUA

COSTA RICA

CENTRAL
AMERICA

PANAMA

CANAL (to U.S.)
ZONE

Panama Canal

CARIBBEAN SEA

VENEZUELA

COLOMBIA

ECUADOR

PERU

SOUTH
AMERICA

BRAZIL

BOLIVIA

Galápagos
Islands
(Ecuadoran)

Equator

Greenwich

West of

Longitude

PACIFIC

O C E A N

MEXICO

Plains

P L A I N S

Tropic of Cancer

20°

10°

0°

10°

70°

80°

90°

100°

110°

120°

130°

30°

20°

10°

0°

10°

Map of
NORTH AMERICA
SCALE OF MILES

0   200   400   600   800

⊕ Capitals of Countries
• Cities
▪▪▪ Boundaries of Countries
▲ Mountain Peaks
△ Canals

Water
Lowlands
Depression
Highlands
Mountains

Copyright by C. S. Hammond & Co., N.Y.

73

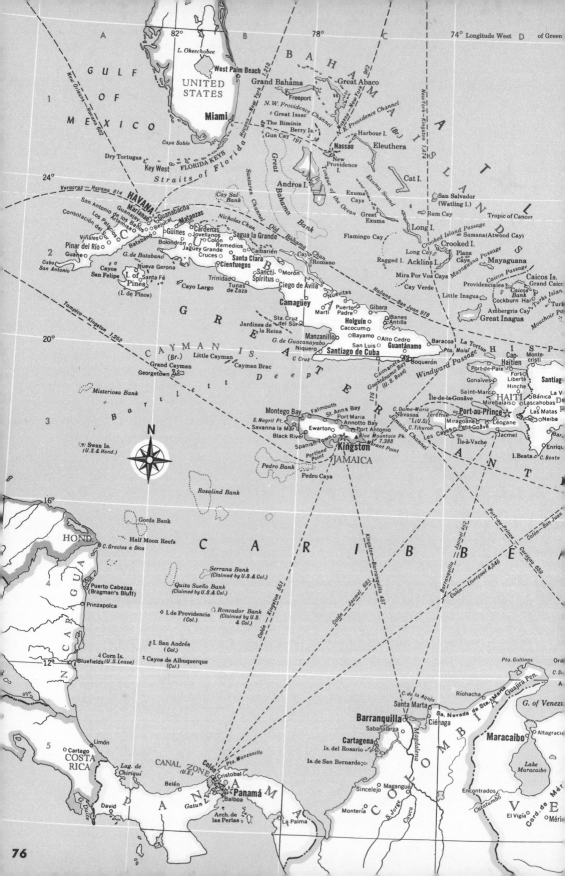

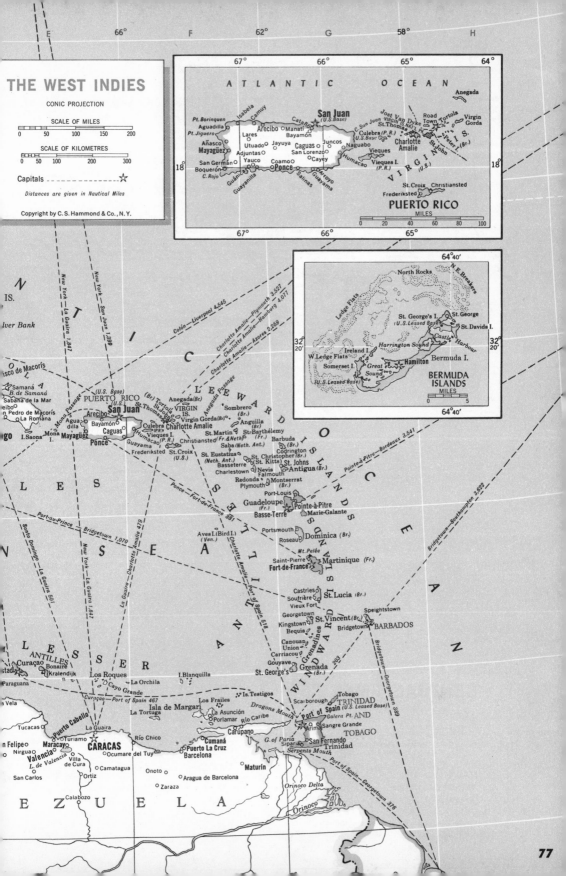

THE WEST INDIES

CONIC PROJECTION

SCALE OF MILES

0   50   100   150   200

SCALE OF KILOMETRES

0   50   100   200   300

Capitals - - - - - - - - ☆

Distances are given in Nautical Miles

Copyright by C. S. Hammond & Co., N. Y.

PUERTO RICO

ATLANTIC OCEAN

Pt. Borinquen
Aguadilla
Pt. Jiguero
Añasco
Mayagüez
San Germán
Boquerón
C. Rojo

Isabela
Lares
Adjuntas
Yauco
Guánica

Camuy
Utuado
Jayuya
Coamo

Arecibo
Manatí
Bayamón

Cataño
San Juan
(U.S. Base)

Caguas
San Lorenzo
Cayey
Salinas
Ponce
Guayanilla
Guayama

Juncos
Naguabo
Humacao
Arroyo

Jost Van Dyke
St. John
(Br.)
Road
Town
Tortola
Virgin
Gorda

San Juan VIRGIN (U.S.)
St. Thomas (U.S.)
Culebra (P.R.)
(U.S. Base)
Charlotte
Amalie
Vieques
Vieques I.
(P.R.)

VIRGIN IS.

Anegada

St. Croix   Christiansted
Frederiksted

PUERTO RICO

MILES
0   20   40   60   80   100

BERMUDA ISLANDS

North Rocks
N.E. Breakers

Ledge Flats
St. George's I.
(U.S. Leased Base)
St. George
St. Davids I.

W. Ledge Flats
Ireland I.
Harrington Sound
Castle Harbour

Somerset I.
Great
Sound
Hamilton
Bermuda I.

U.S. Leased Base

BERMUDA ISLANDS

MILES
0   5

LESSER ANTILLES

New York - San Juan 1,399
New York - La Guaira 1,847
La Guaira 1,847

Colón - Liverpool 4,545
Charlotte Amalie - Plymouth 3,527
Charlotte Amalie - Hamburg 4,077
Charlotte Amalie - Azores 2,259

Iver Bank

isco de Macorís
Samaná
B. de Samaná
Sabana de la Mar
eibo
n Pedro de Macorís
La Romana
I. Saona
go
Mona Passage

PUERTO RICO
(U.S.)
Arecibo
Bayamón
Mayagüez
Ponce
Guayama
San Juan
Caguas
Humacao

Mona Passage

(Br.) Tortola
St. Thomas (U.S.)
Virgin Gorda (Br.)
Culebra
(P.R.)
Vieques I.
(P.R.)

Anegada (Br.)
VIRGIN
IS.
Charlotte Amalie
Christiansted (Fr. & Neth.)
St. Croix
(U.S.)

Sombrero
(Br.)
Anguilla
(Br.)
St. Martin
(Fr. & Neth.)
Saba (Neth. Ant.)
St. Eustatius
(Neth. Ant.)
St. Barthélemy
(Fr.)
Barbuda
(Br.)

Codrington
St. Christopher (Br.)
St. Kitts
Basseterre
Charlestown Nevis
Redonda
Plymouth
St. Johns
Antigua
Falmouth
Montserrat
(Br.)

Ponce - Fort-de-France 381

Port-Louis
Guadeloupe
(Fr.)
Basse-Terre
Pointe-à-Pitre
Marie-Galante

New York - La Guaira 1,847
Port-au-Prince - Bridgetown 1,070
Santo Domingo - La Guaira 501

La Guaira - Charlotte Amalie 470

Charlotte Amalie - Port of Spain 618

Portsmouth
Avea I. (Bird I.)
(Ven.)
Roseau
Dominica (Br.)

Mt. Pelée
Saint-Pierre
Fort-de-France
Martinique (Fr.)

Castries
Soufrière
Vieux Fort
St. Lucia (Br.)

Georgetown
Kingstown
Bequia
Canouan
Union
Carriacou
Gouyave
St. George's
St. Vincent (Br.)
Bridgetown
Grenadines
Speightstown
BARBADOS

WINDWARD ISLANDS

Pointe-à-Pitre - Bordeaux 3,541

Bridgetown - Southampton 3,692
Bridgetown - Georgetown

Grenada
(Br.)

ANTILLES
Curaçao
Bonaire
Kralendijk

Los Roques
La Orchila
I. Blanquilla
Cayo Grande

Paraguaná
Curaçao - Port of Spain 467
a Vela
Tucacas
n Felipe
Nirguas
Puerto Cabello
Turiamo
La Guaira
Maracay
Valencia
L. de Valencia
CARACAS
Ocumare del Tuy
Villa
de Cura
San Carlos
Camatagua
Ortiz
Calabozo

Los Frailes
La Tortuga

Isla de Margarita
La Asunción
Porlamar

Is. Testigos

Río Caribe
Carúpano
Río Chico
Cumaná
Puerto La Cruz
Barcelona
Onoto
Aragua de Barcelona
Zaraza

Scarborough
Tobago

Dragons Mouth
Sangre Grande
Arima
G. of Paria
San Fernando
Siparia
Serpents Mouth
Trinidad

TRINIDAD
(U.S. Leased Base)
Galeota Pt. AND
Port of Spain
TOBAGO

Bridgetown - Georgetown 389

Port of Spain - Georgetown 376

Maturín

Orinoco Delta

Orinoco

EZUELA

77

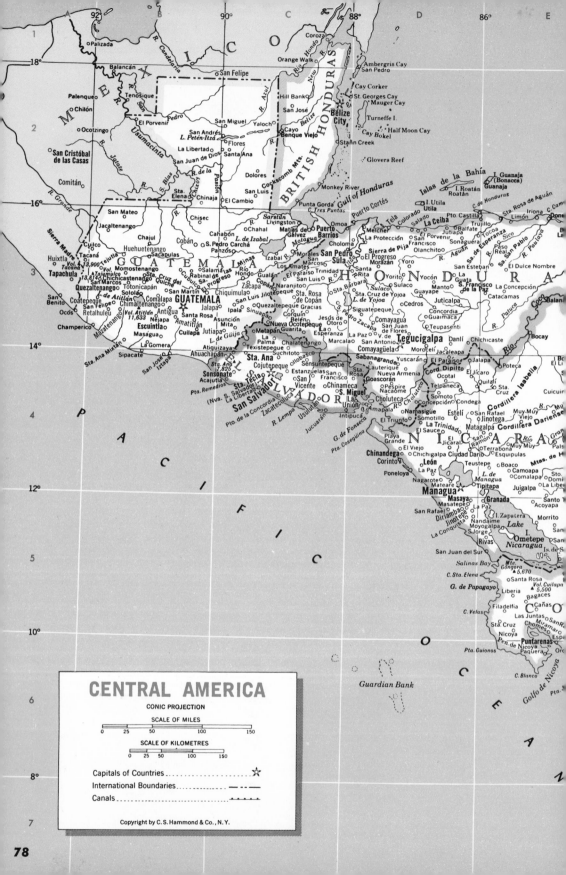

CENTRAL AMERICA

CONIC PROJECTION

SCALE OF MILES

| 0 | 25 | 50 | 100 | 150 |

SCALE OF KILOMETRES

| 0 | 25 | 50 | 100 | 150 |

Capitals of Countries .... ☆

International Boundaries .... — ∙ — ∙ —

Canals .... ∙∙∙∙∙∙∙

Copyright by C.S. Hammond & Co., N.Y.

78

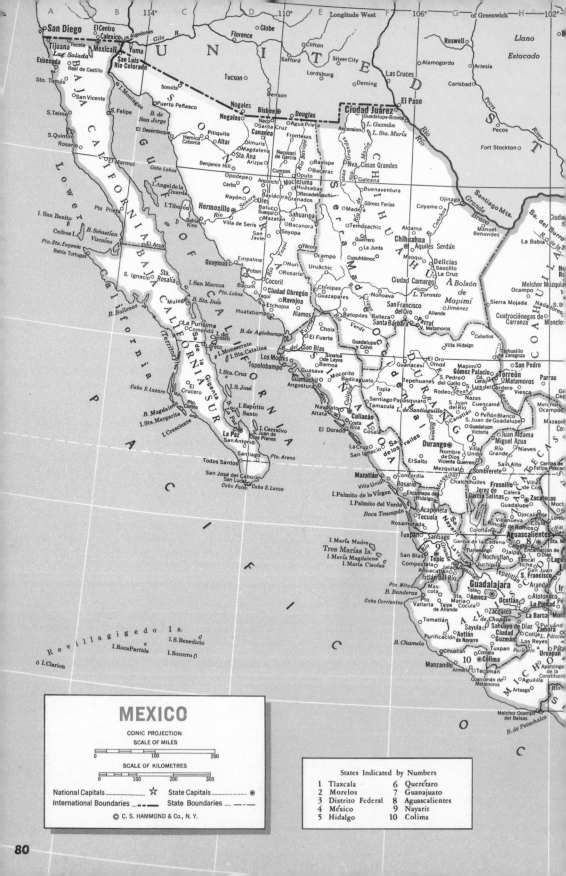

MEXICO

CONIC PROJECTION

SCALE OF MILES

0   100   200

SCALE OF KILOMETRES

0   100   200   300

National Capitals .... ☆   State Capitals .... ◉

International Boundaries ...... ---   State Boundaries ...... -·-·-

© C. S. HAMMOND & Co., N.Y.

States Indicated by Numbers

1	Tlaxcala	6	Querétaro
2	Morelos	7	Guanajuato
3	Distrito Federal	8	Aguascalientes
4	México	9	Nayarit
5	Hidalgo	10	Colima

180° ASIA 170° 160° 150° 140° 130° 120° 17

BERING U.S.S.R. 70° 80° ARCTIC OCEAN

St. Lawrence Island Bering Strait

SEA 60° Point Barrow BEAUFORT SEA Queen Eli

Nome BROOKS RANGE Banks Island McClure Strait North Magnetic Po

UNITED STATES Yukon River Amundsen Gulf Viscount Me Sound

ALASKA Mt. McKinley Fairbanks DISTRICT

ALASKA RANGE Anchorage YUKON Coppermine Victoria Island W Is

Alaska Peninsula Dawson TERRITORY MACKENZIE MTS Great Bear Lake Port Radium NORTHWEST

Kodiak Island Gulf of Alaska Mt. Logan Whitehorse Mackenzie River DISTRICT OF MACKENZIE Yellowknife

PACIFIC Alexander Juneau Fort Providence Great Slave Lake

Archipelago COAST Fort Nelson Fort Smith Uranium City

50° Prince Rupert Hazelton ROCKY BRITISH Dawson Creek Peace River McMurray Lake Athabasca Rein Lake

Queen Charlotte Islands Kitimat Prince George River Peace River Flin

OCEAN MOUNTAINS COLUMBIA ALBERTA SASKATCHEWAN The

Vancouver Island Fraser Edmonton N. Saskatchewan Prince Albert Saskatoon

Kamloops Calgary R. Regina Win

Victoria Vancouver Medicine Hat S. Saskatchewan R. Moose Jaw

Cape Flattery Seattle Lethbridge Missouri

Portland Columbia Spokane MOUNTAINS Helena Bismarck

40° CASCADE RANGE Snake River UNITED ST

Boise River Pierre

130° 120° Longitude 110° West of 100

82

80° 70° 60° 50° 40° 30° 20°

GREENLAND
(Danish)

ICELAND

70°

Reykjavik

Ellesmere Island

Thule

60°

Islands

BAFFIN

Devon Island

Lancaster Sound

BAY

FRANKLIN

Baffin Island

Arctic Circle

Gulf of Boothia

Davis Strait

ATLANTIC

OCEAN

Foxe
Basin

Godthaab

Cape
Farewell

RICT

Frobisher Bay

T E R R I T O R I E S

Southampton
Island

Hudson Strait

VATIN

Chesterfield
Inlet

Ungava
Peninsula

Nain

Fort
Chimo

Battle
Harbour

50°

Port Harrison

Churchill

HUDSON

Schefferville

Goose Airport

Newfoundland

Port
Nelson

BAY

Belcher
Islands

Grand
Falls

Gander

St.
John's

OBA

Severn River

Fort George

Fort George

James

Bay

Lake
Mistassini

QUÉBEC

Seven
Islands

Anticosti
Island

Corner
Brook

St. Pierre &
Miquelon
(French)

Moosonee

Gulf of
St. Lawrence

Gaspé
Peninsula

PRINCE
EDWARD
ISLAND

Charlottetown

Sydney

Cape Breton
Island

O N T A R I O

Lake Nipigon

Kapuskasing

Rouyn

Chicoutimi

NEW
BRUNSWICK

Moncton

Sable Island

Kenora

Lake of
the Woods

Timmins

Québec

Fredericton

Saint
John

Halifax

Port
Arthur

Trois
Rivières

St. Lawrence River

Sherbrooke

NOVA SCOTIA

Fort William

Lake Superior

Sudbury

Montréal

Cape Sable

Duluth

Sault-
Ste-Marie

North
Bay

Ottawa

Cornwall

APPALACHIAN MTS.

Yarmouth

40°

St. Paul

Mississippi R.

Lake Michigan

Lake Huron

Toronto

Lake
Ontario

Boston

Greenwich 90°

Milwaukee

Detroit
Windsor

Lake Erie

Buffalo

New York

70°

80°

Copyright by C. S. HAMMOND & Co. N. Y.

83

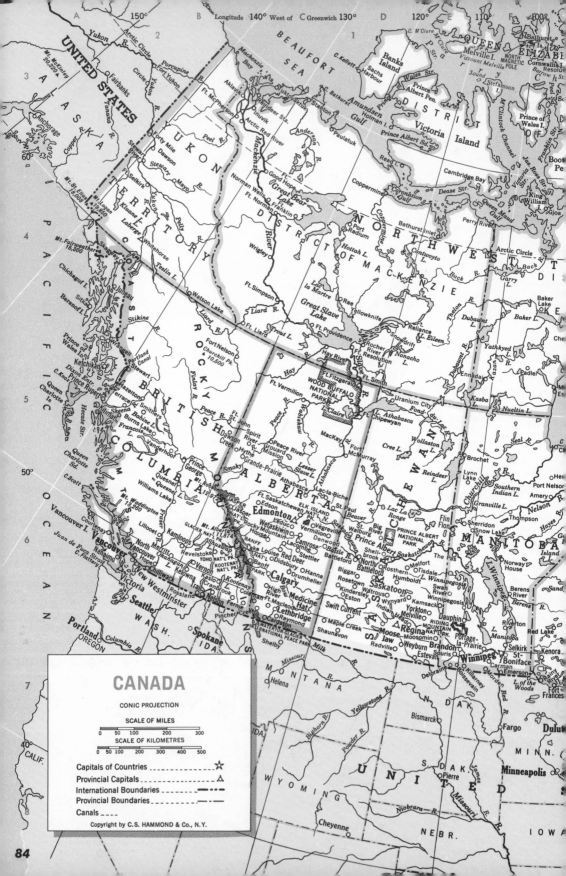

CANADA

CONIC PROJECTION

SCALE OF MILES
0 50 100   200   300

SCALE OF KILOMETRES
0 50 100   200   300   400   500

Capitals of Countries _ _ _ _ _ _ _ ☆
Provincial Capitals _ _ _ _ _ _ _ _ △
International Boundaries _ _ _ _ _ _
Provincial Boundaries _ _ _ _ _ _ _
Canals _ _ _ _

Copyright by C.S. HAMMOND & Co., N.Y.

84

GREENLAND

BAFFIN BAY

DAVIS STRAIT

QUEEN ELIZABETH ISLANDS
Scale of Miles
0 50 100 200

ARCTIC OCEAN

UNITED STATES
C. Columbia
Alert
ELLESMERE ISLAND
Meighen I.
Axel Heiberg
Peary Chan.
SVERDRUP ISLANDS
Brock I.
Borden I.
Mackenzie King I.
Prince Patrick I.
Eglinton I.
Ringnes I.
Cornwall I.
M'Clure Str.
PARRY ISLANDS
Melville Island
Banks I.
Viscount Melville Sd.
Resolute
Bathurst
Cornwallis I.
Devon I.
Jones Sd.
Lancaster Sd.

FOXE BASIN

BAFFIN ISLAND

HUDSON STRAIT

Melville Pen.

Foxe Pen.

Cumberland Pen.
Cumberland Sound

Frobisher Bay

Resolution I.

Ungava Peninsula

Ungava Bay

ATLANTIC OCEAN

NEWFOUNDLAND

QUEBEC

HUDSON BAY

James Bay

ONTARIO

Gulf of St. Lawrence

PRINCE EDWARD ISLAND

NEW BRUNSWICK

NOVA SCOTIA

Halifax

MONTRÉAL

Ottawa

TORONTO

MAINE

N.H.

VT.

MASS.

BOSTON

NEW YORK

DETROIT

Buffalo

Cleveland

P A.

N.J.

ATLANTIC OCEAN

MARITIME PROVINCES

SCALE OF MILES

0 10 20 30 40 50

Provincial Capitals .... ⊛   Provincial Boundaries ── ∙ ──
County Seats .... ◉   County Boundaries ── ── ──
International Boundaries ── ∙∙ ──

Copyright by C.S. Hammond & Co., N.Y.

86

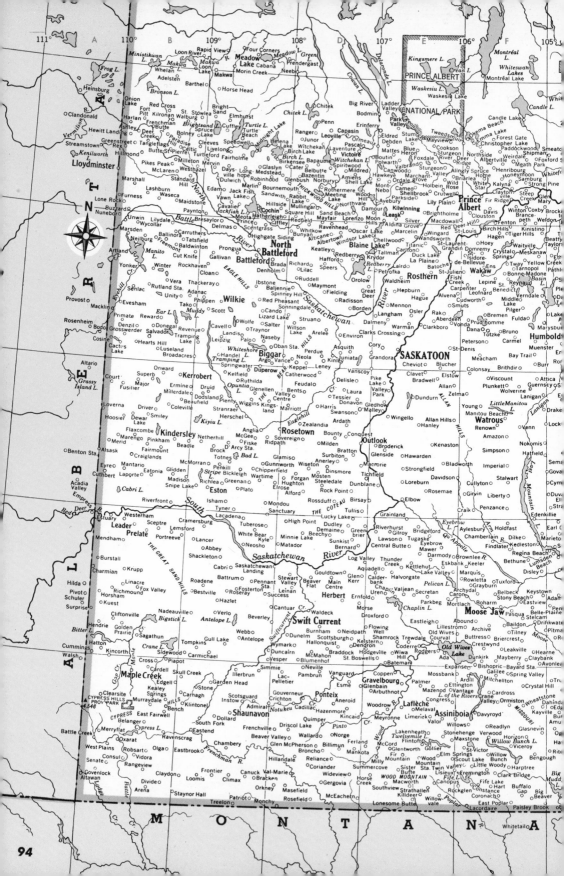

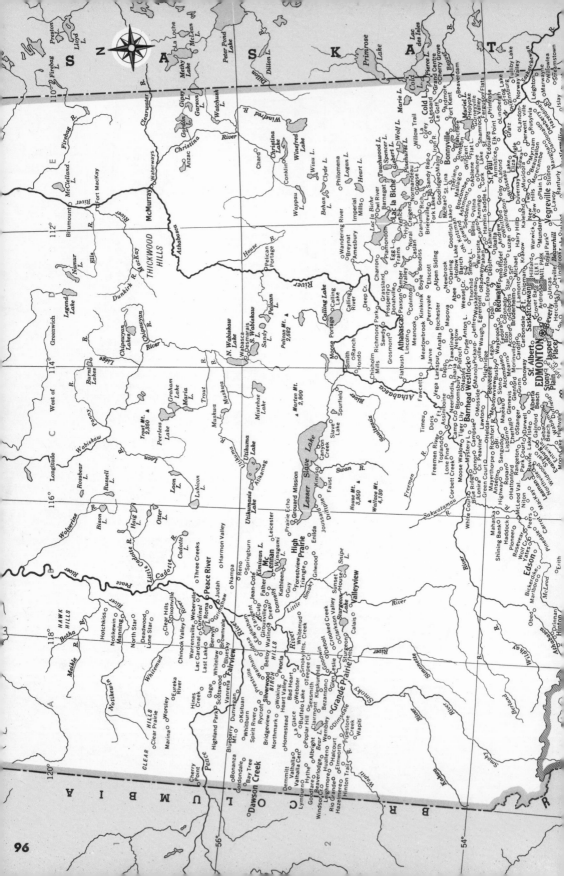

ALBERTA
SOUTHERN PART

SCALE OF MILES

Provincial Capital ⊛
International Boundaries
Provincial Boundaries

Copyright by C. S. Hammond & Co. N. Y.

ALBERTA
NORTHERN PART

SCALE OF MILES

BRITISH COLUMBIA
SOUTHERN PART
SCALE OF MILES

| 0 | 15 | 30 | | 90 | 120 |

Provincial Capital ----------⊕
State Capital ----------✸
International Boundaries -----
Provincial Boundaries -----

Copyright by C. S. Hammond & Co., N.Y.

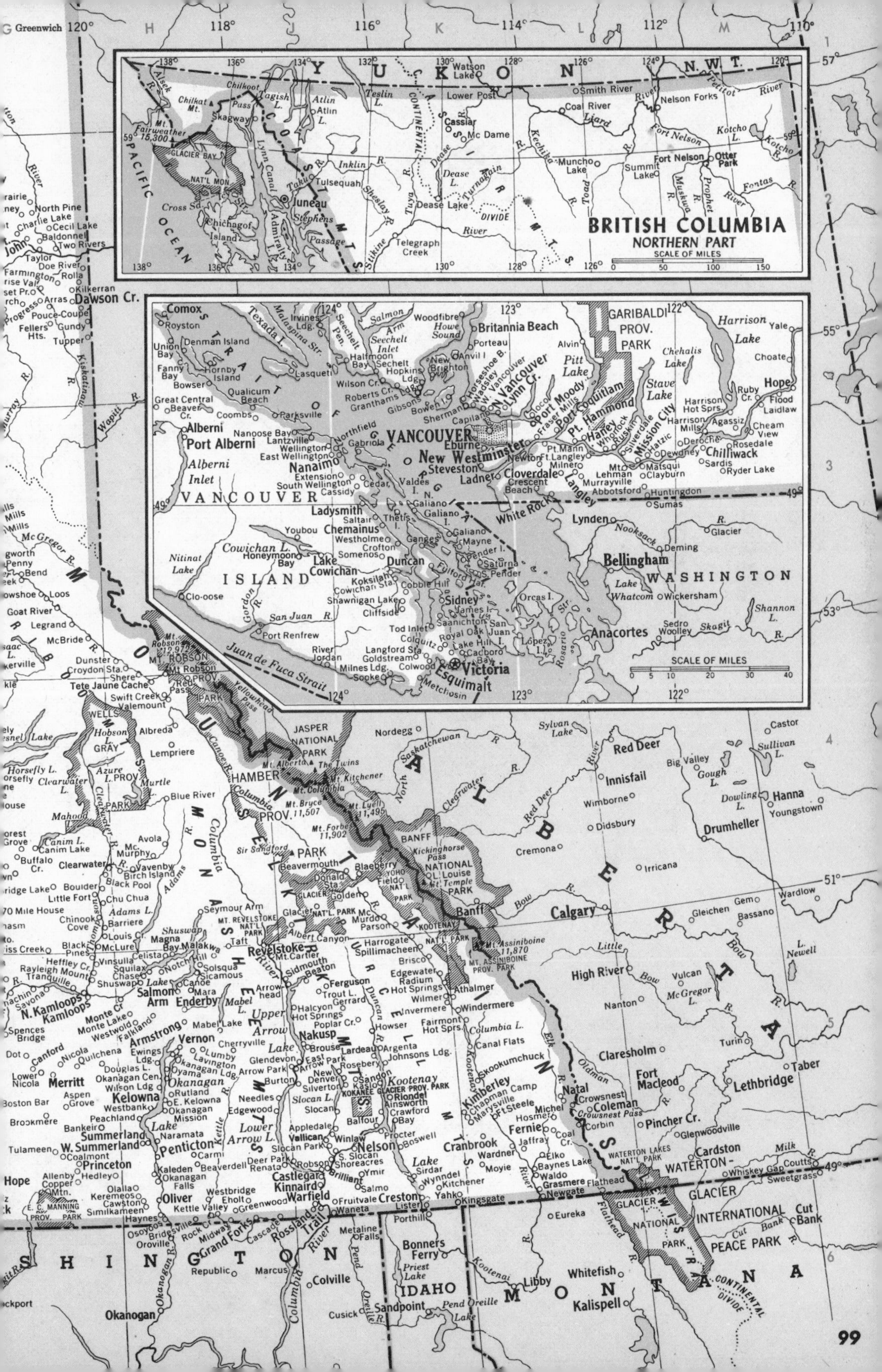
BRITISH COLUMBIA
NORTHERN PART
SCALE OF MILES
0 50 100 150
YUKON
N.W.T.
PACIFIC OCEAN
GLACIER BAY NAT'L MON.
Mt. Fairweather 15,300
Skagway
Juneau
Atlin
Watson Lake
Lower Post
Cassiar
Mc Dame
Dease Lake
Telegraph Creek
Smith River
Coal River
Nelson Forks
Fort Nelson
Muncho Lake
Summit Lake
Otter Park
CONTINENTAL DIVIDE
Liard
Stikine R.
VANCOUVER
New Westminster
North Vancouver
Victoria
Esquimalt
Nanaimo
Port Alberni
Alberni
Ladysmith
Chemainus
Duncan
Sidney
Comox
Britannia Beach
Squamish
Port Moody
Port Coquitlam
Pt. Hammond
Haney
Mission City
Chilliwack
Hope
Harrison Lake
Pitt Lake
Stave Lake
GARIBALDI PROV. PARK
Steveston
Ladner
Cloverdale
Langley
White Rock
Abbotsford
Lynden
Bellingham
Anacortes
WASHINGTON
VANCOUVER ISLAND
STRAIT OF GEORGIA
Juan de Fuca Strait
Cowichan L.
Port Renfrew
SCALE OF MILES
0 5 10 20 30 40
Greenwich 120° 118° 116° 114° 112° 110°
Dawson Cr.
Tete Jaune Cache
MT. ROBSON PROV. PARK
Mt. Robson 12,972
JASPER NATIONAL PARK
HAMBER PROV. PARK
Mt. Columbia
Mt. Forbes 11,902
BANFF NATIONAL PARK
YOHO NAT'L PARK
GLACIER NAT'L PARK
MT. REVELSTOKE NAT'L PARK
KOOTENAY NAT'L PARK
Mt. Assiniboine 11,870
WELLS GRAY PROV. PARK
Banff
Calgary
Red Deer
Innisfail
Drumheller
Hanna
High River
Claresholm
Fort Macleod
Lethbridge
Taber
Cardston
Pincher Cr.
Coleman
Crowsnest Pass
Fernie
Cranbrook
Kimberley
Creston
Nelson
Trail
Rossland
Castlegar
Kinnaird
Nakusp
Revelstoke
Golden
Salmon Arm
Enderby
Armstrong
Vernon
Kelowna
Penticton
Summerland
Oliver
Princeton
Merritt
Kamloops
N. Kamloops
Grand Forks
Greenwood
KOKANEE GLACIER PROV. PARK
E. C. MANNING PROV. PARK
WATERTON LAKES NAT'L PARK
WATERTON-GLACIER INTERNATIONAL PEACE PARK
GLACIER NATIONAL PARK
ALBERTA
MONTANA
IDAHO
WASHINGTON
ROCKY MTS.
SELKIRK MTS.
MONASHEE MTS.
PURCELL MTS.
CARIBOO MTS.
Columbia R.
Kootenay L.
Okanagan Lake
Arrow L.
Bonners Ferry
Sandpoint
Kalispell
Whitefish
Libby
Colville
Okanogan
Cut Bank
Sweetgrass

Map of
UNITED STATES
LAMBERT CONFORMAL CONIC PROJECTION
Copyright by C. S. HAMMOND & Co., N.Y.
SCALE OF MILES
0   50   100   200   300

Capitals of Countries
State and Provincial Capitals
International Boundaries
State Boundaries
Provincial Boundaries

Copyright by C. S. Hammond & Co., N.Y.

APPROXIMATE ELEVATIONS
10,000 ft.
5,000 ft.
2,000 ft.
1,000 ft.
500 ft.
Sea level
Depression

Longitude 90° West of Greenwich

101

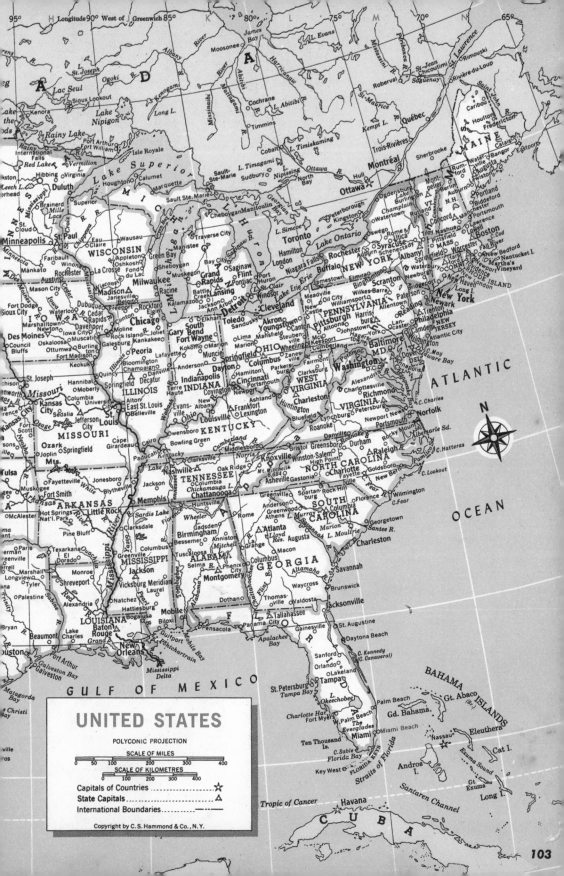

UNITED STATES

POLYCONIC PROJECTION

SCALE OF MILES

0 50 100   200   300   400

SCALE OF KILOMETRES

0   100   200   300   400

Capitals of Countries .... ☆
State Capitals .... △
International Boundaries .... ———

Copyright by C. S. Hammond & Co., N.Y.

103

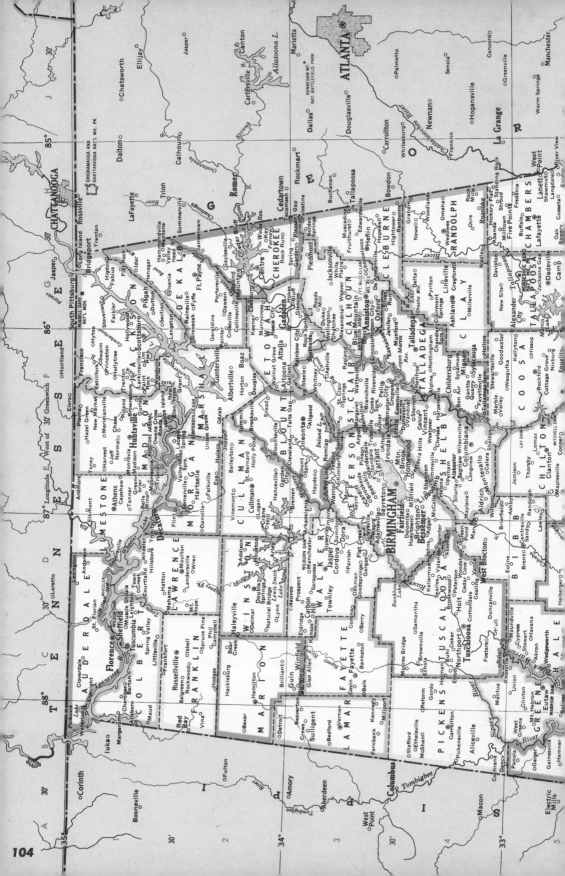

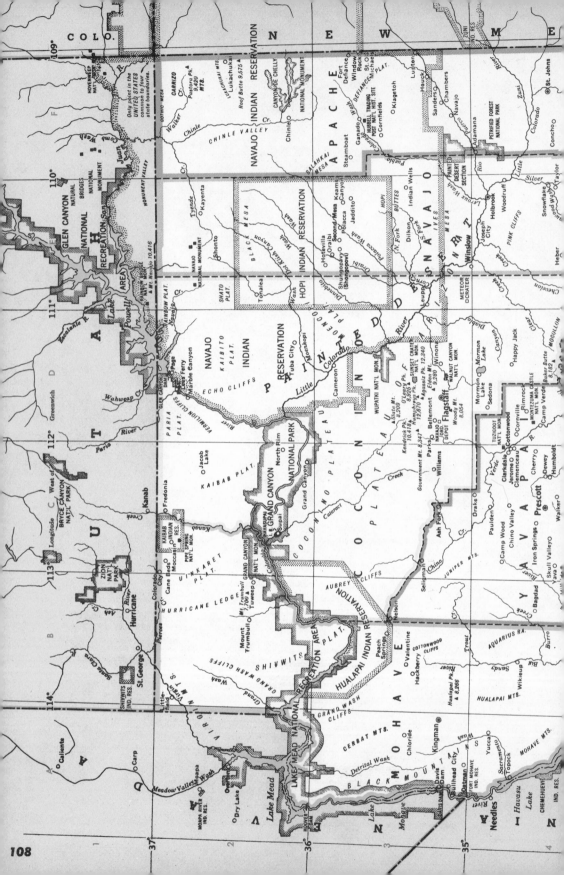

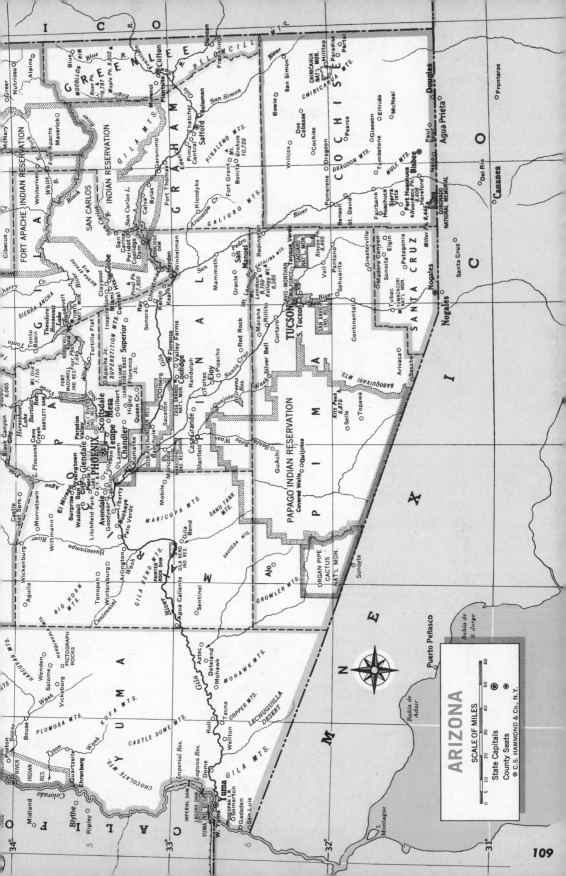

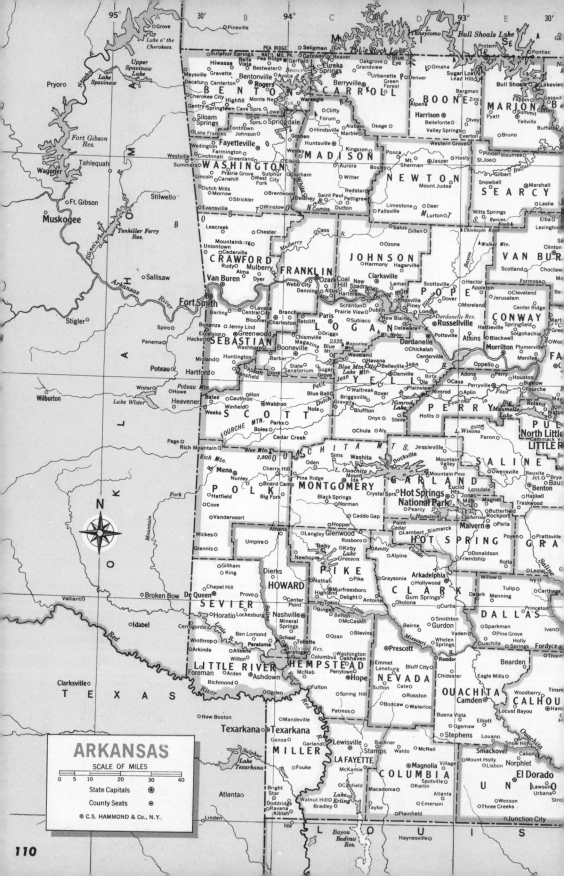

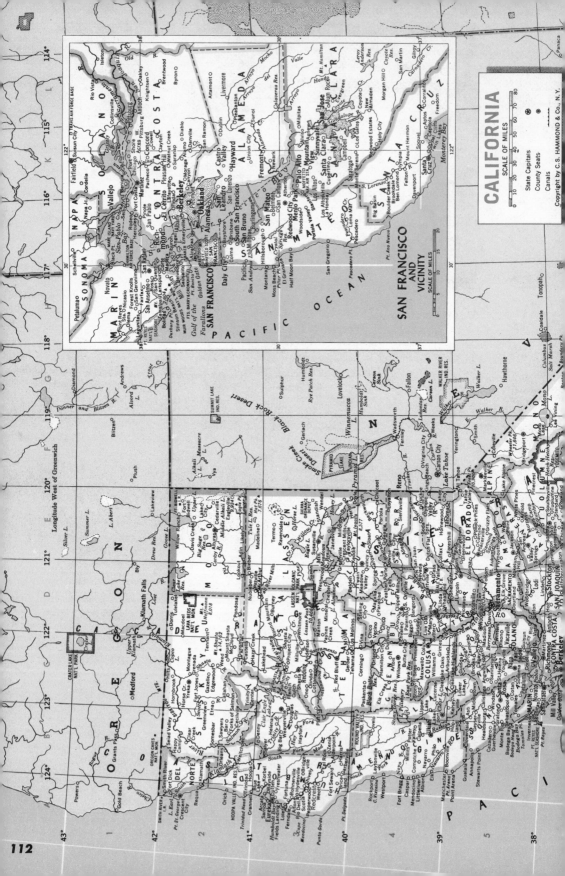

COLORADO

SCALE OF MILES

0 5 10 20 30 40

State Capitals ⊛   County Seats ◉

Canals

Copyright by C. S. Hammond & Co., N.Y.

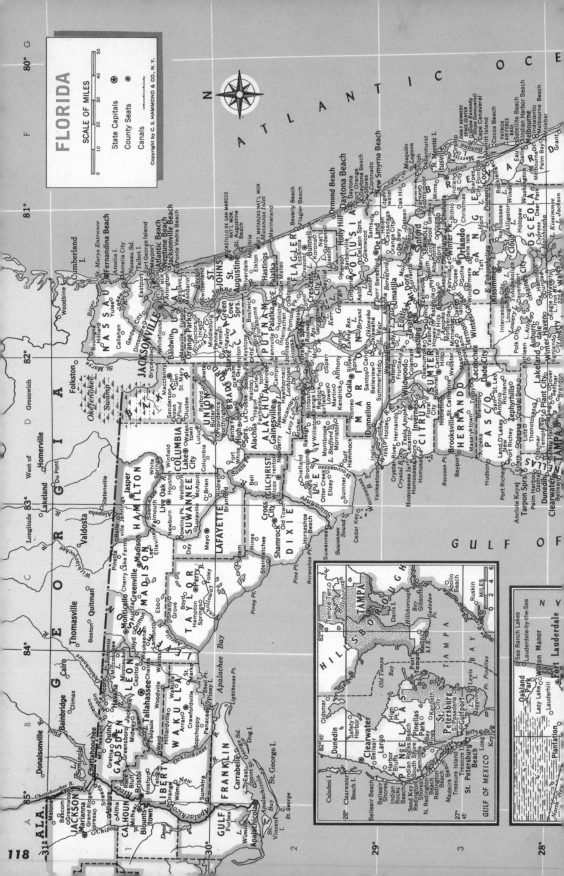

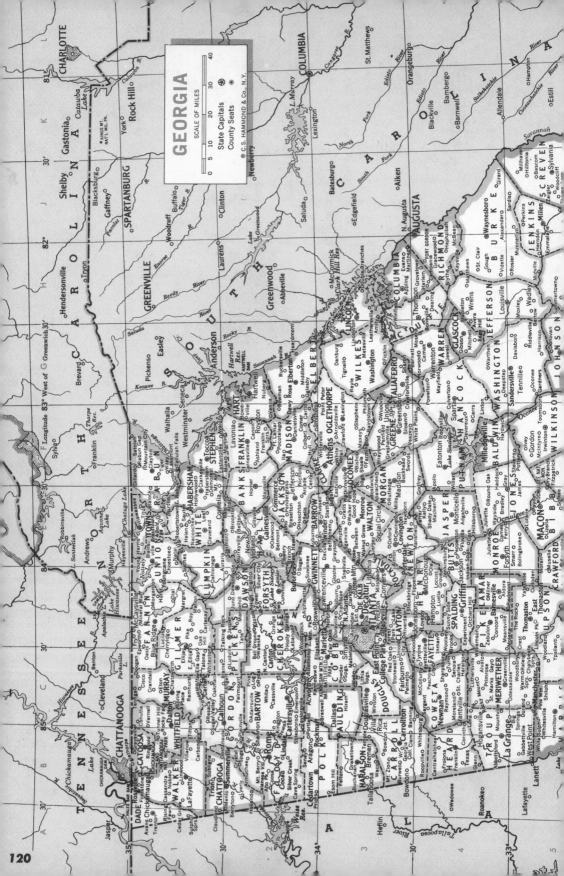

GEORGIA

SCALE OF MILES

State Capitals ⊛
County Seats ◉

C.S. HAMMOND & Co., N.Y.

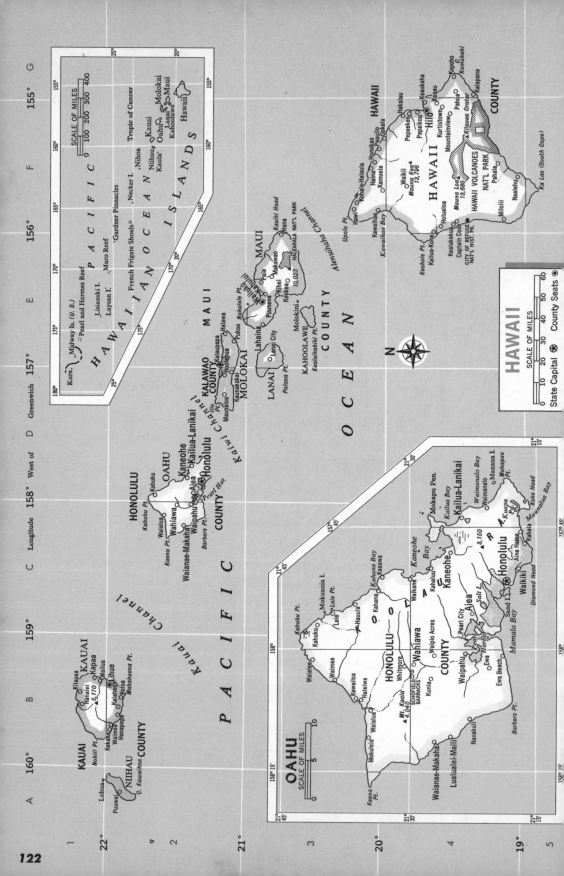

IDAHO

SCALE OF MILES

0   20   40   60   80

⊛ State Capitals
◉ County Seats

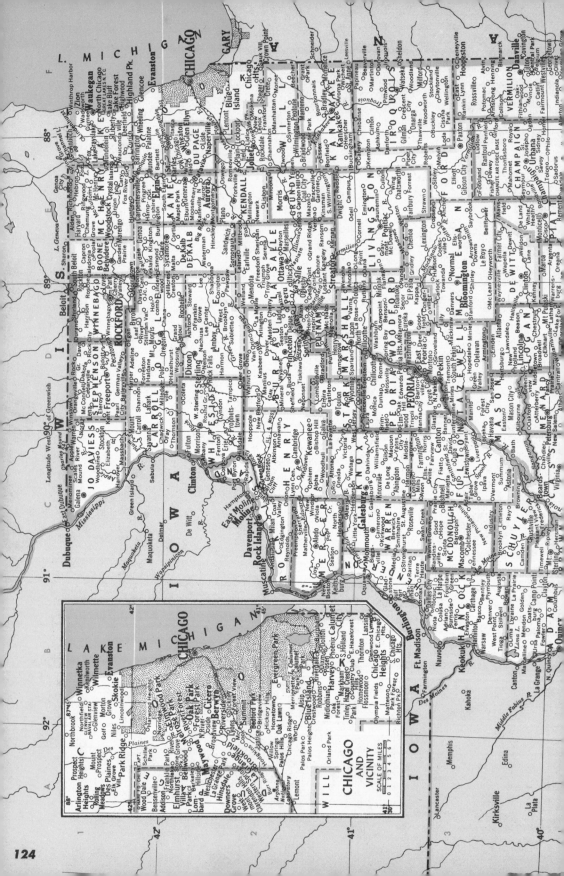

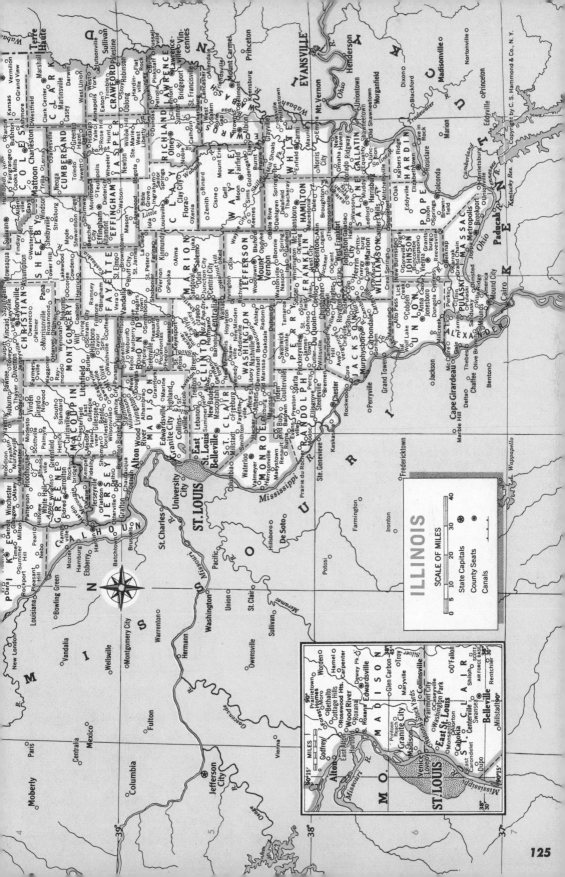

ILLINOIS

SCALE OF MILES

State Capitals
County Seats
Canals

125

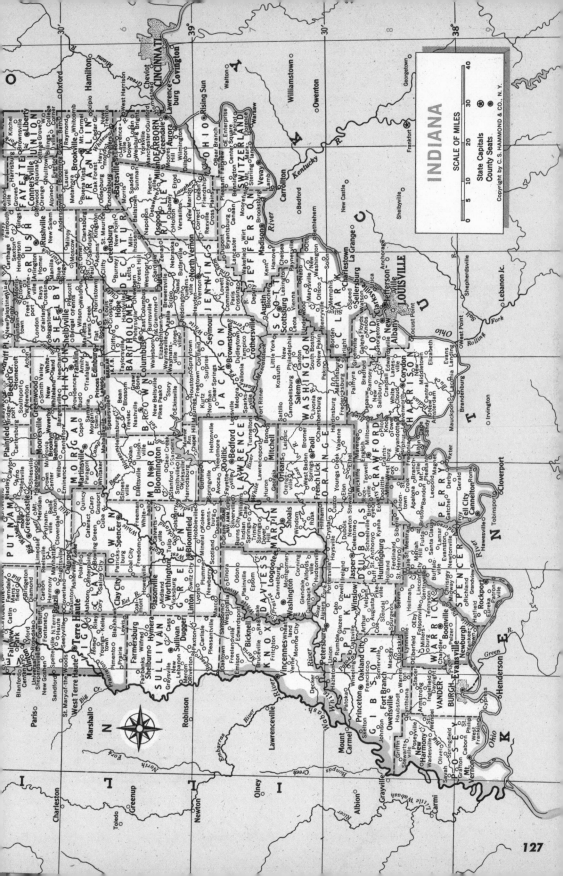

129

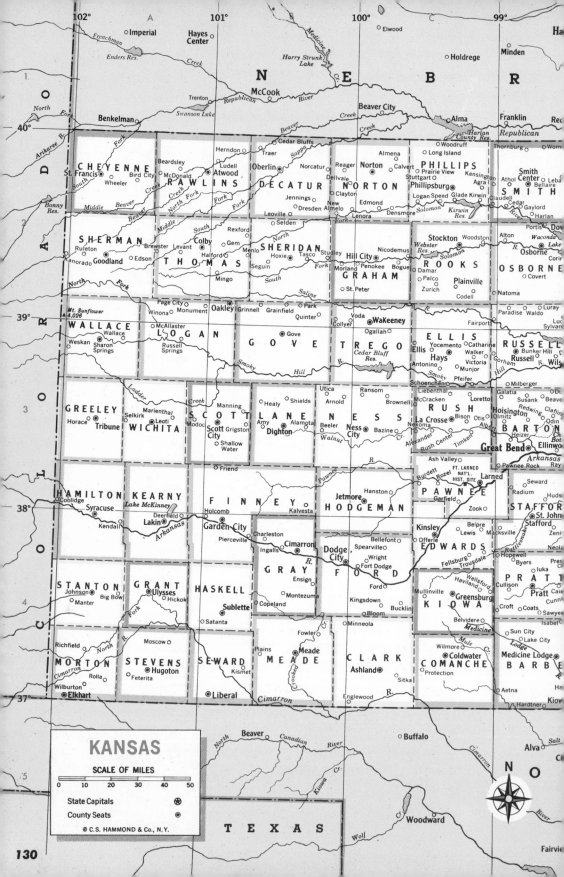

WESTERN PART OF KENTUCKY

Same scale as main map

Copyright by C. S. HAMMOND & Co., N.Y.

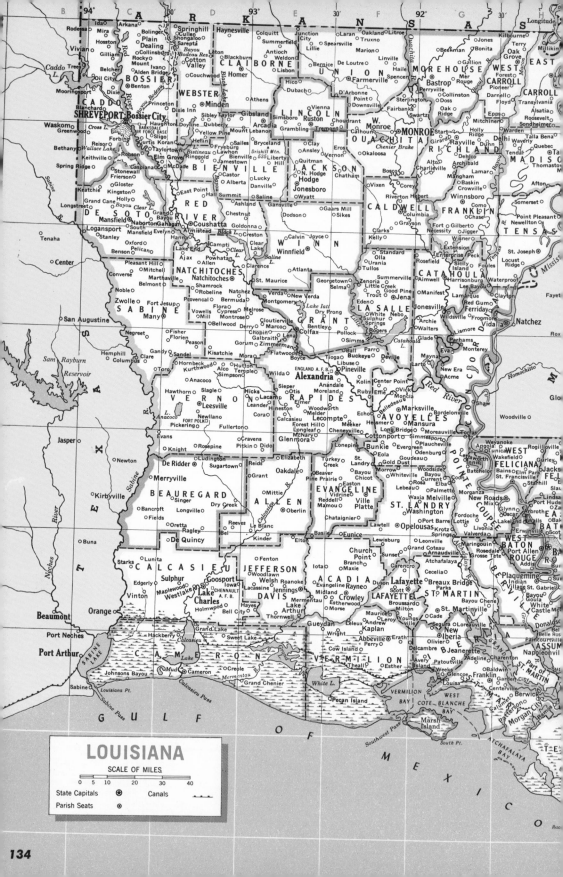

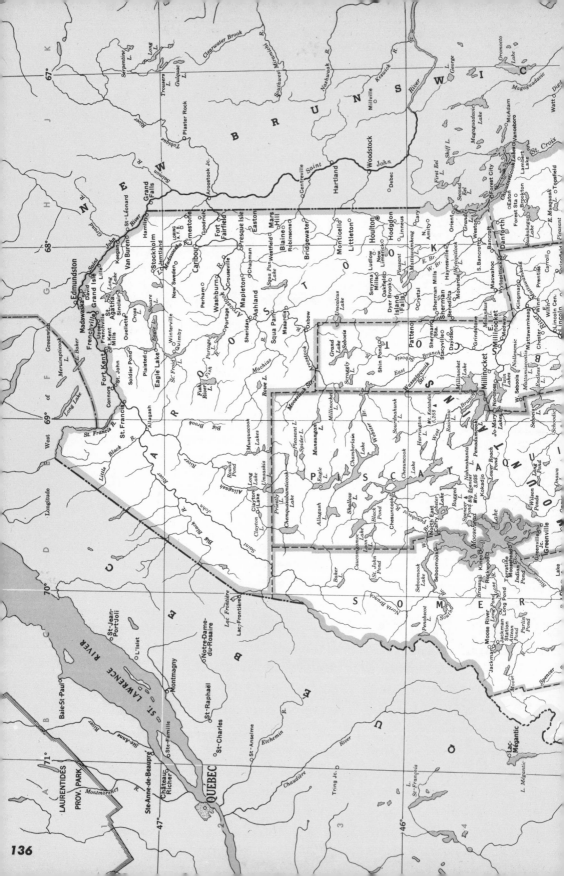

MAINE

SCALE OF MILES

State Capitals ⊛
County Seats ⊙

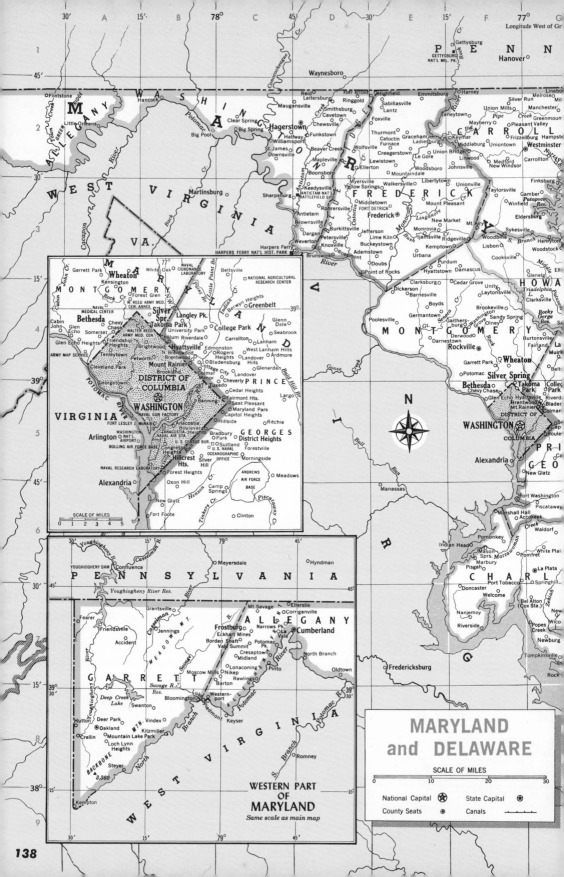

MARYLAND and DELAWARE

SCALE OF MILES

| National Capital | ✪ | State Capital | ✪ |
| County Seats | ⊛ | Canals | |

WESTERN PART OF MARYLAND
Same scale as main map

139

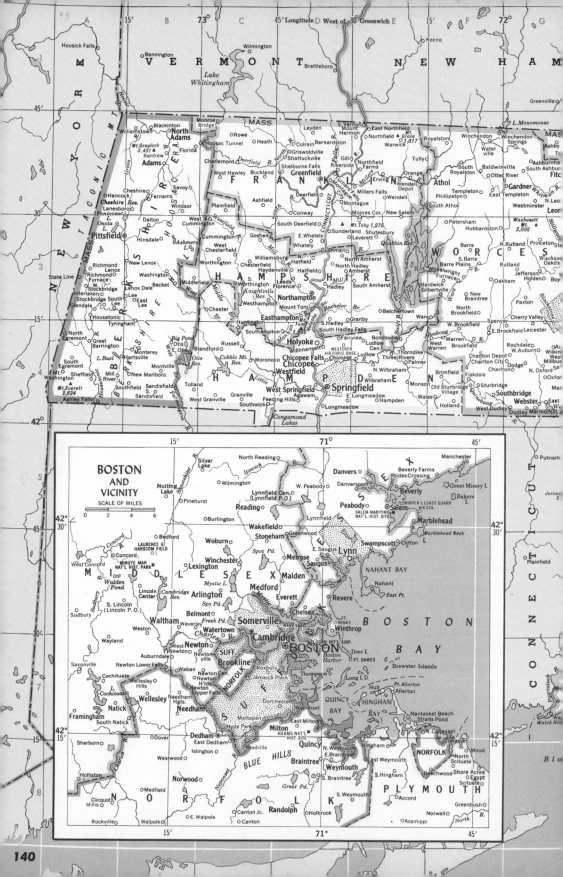

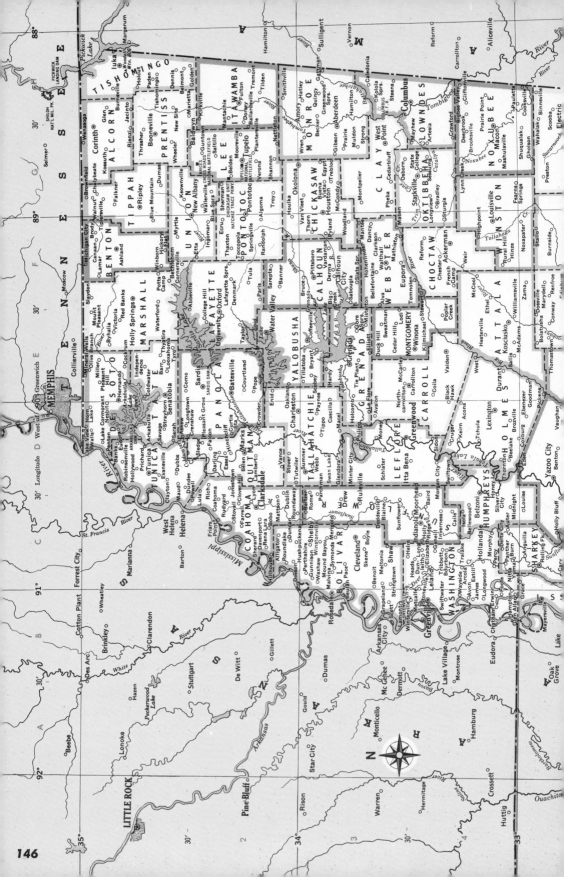

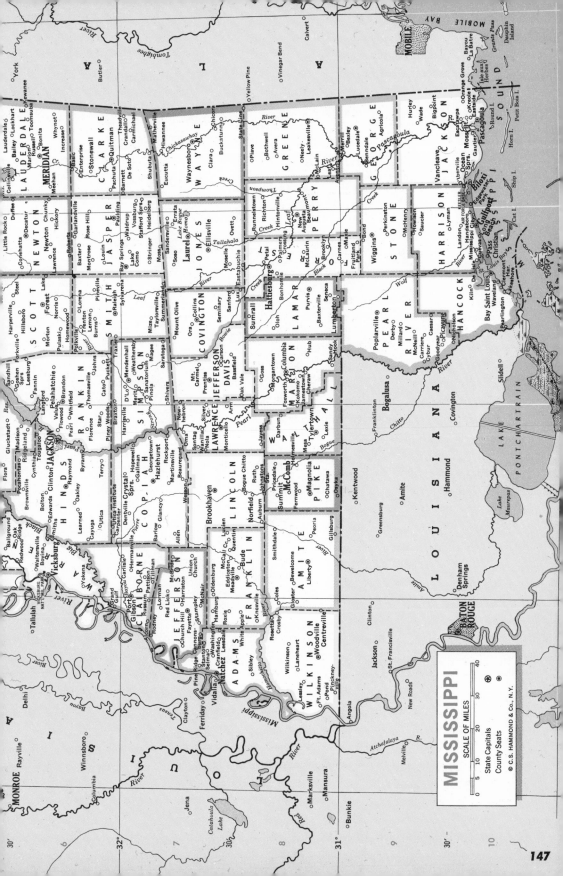

MISSISSIPPI

SCALE OF MILES

0 5 10 20 30 40

⊕ State Capitals
◉ County Seats

© C. S. HAMMOND & Co., N.Y.

MONTANA

SCALE OF MILES

0 10 20 40 60 80

State Capitals

County Seats

150

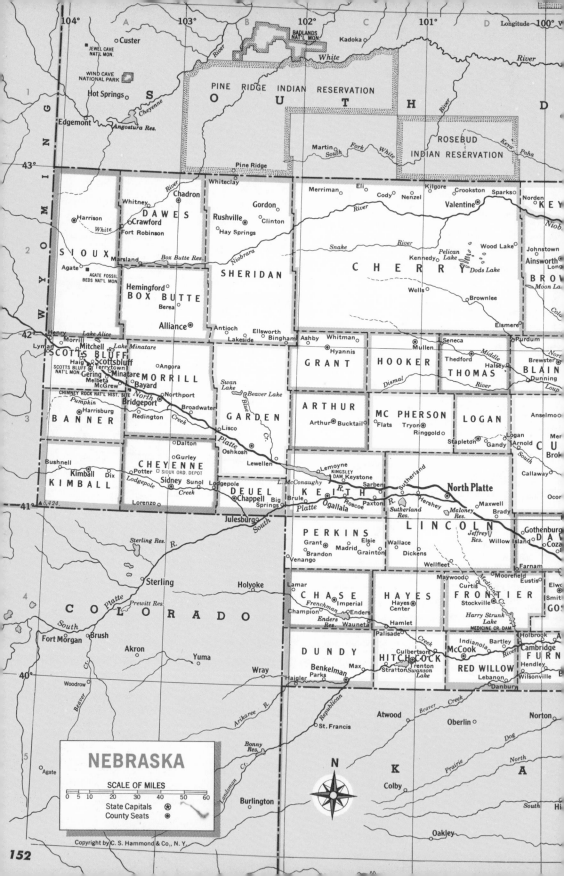

NEBRASKA

SCALE OF MILES

0 5 10   20   30   40   50   60

State Capitals ⊛
County Seats ⊙

Copyright by C. S. Hammond & Co., N. Y.

152

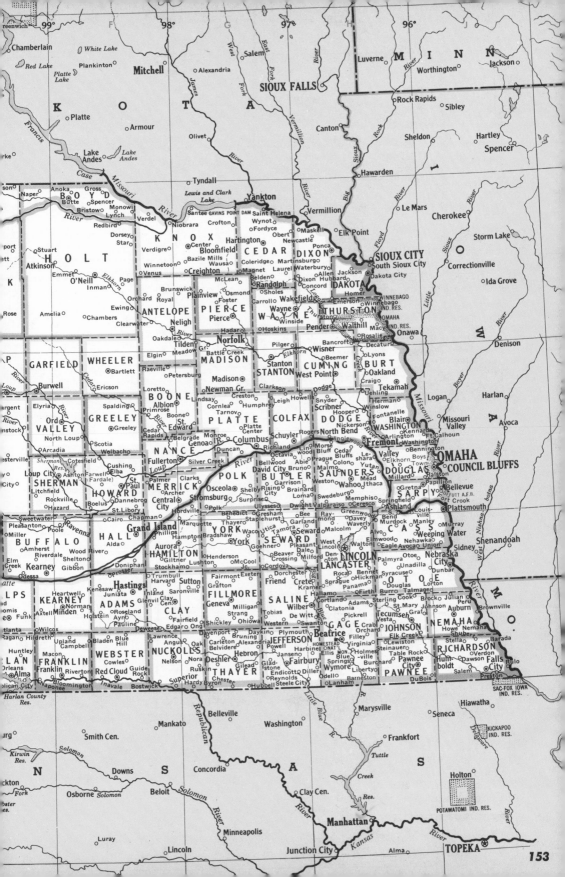

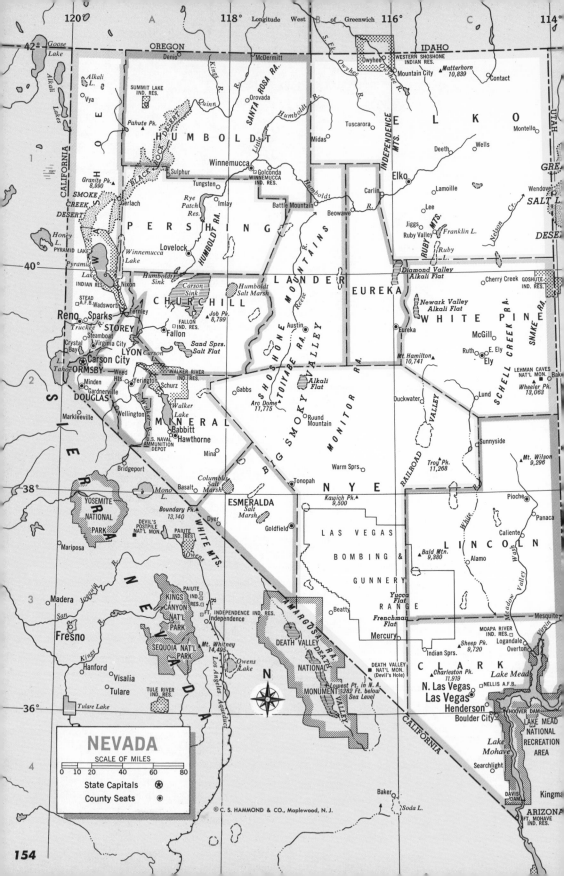

NEVADA
SCALE OF MILES
0 10 20 40 60 80

⊛ State Capitals
⊙ County Seats

© C. S. HAMMOND & CO., Maplewood, N.J.

154

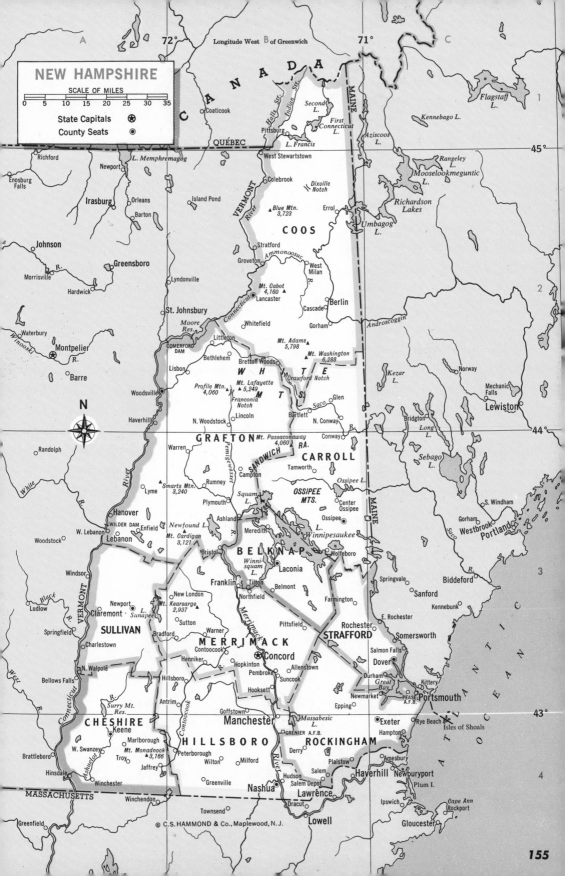

NEW HAMPSHIRE

SCALE OF MILES

0 5 10 15 20 25 30 35

⊛ State Capitals
◉ County Seats

CANADA

A — 72° — Longitude West B of Greenwich — 71° — C

QUÉBEC

Coaticook
Richford
Enosburg Falls
Newport
L. Memphremagog
Irasburg
Orleans
Barton

Johnson
Morrisville
Hardwick
Greensboro

Waterbury
Winooski R.
Montpelier ⊛
Barre

Island Pond
Lyndonville

St. Johnsbury

Woodsville
Haverhill

Randolph
Woodstock
W. Lebanon
Lebanon
Hanover
Enfield
WILDER DAM

Windsor
Ludlow
Springfield
Newport
Claremont
L. Sunapee

Charlestown
N. Walpole
Bellows Falls

Brattleboro
Hinsdale

MASSACHUSETTS

Pittsburg
Halls Str. Indian Str.
Second L.
First Connecticut L.
L. Francis
West Stewartstown
Colebrook
Dixville Notch
Blue Mtn. 3,723
Errol

Stratford
Groveton
West Milan
Cascade
Berlin
Gorham

COOS

Lancaster
Mt. Cabot 4,160
Whitefield
Moore Res.
COMERFORD DAM
Littleton
Bethlehem
Bretton Woods
Mt. Adams 5,798
Mt. Washington 6,288
Crawford Notch
Lisbon
Profile Mtn. 4,060
Mt. Lafayette 5,249
Franconia Notch
N. Woodstock
Lincoln
Bartlett
N. Conway
Conway

WHITE MTS.

GRAFTON
Warren
SANDWICH RA.
CARROLL
Mt. Passaconaway 4,060
Rumney
Tamworth
Campton
OSSIPEE MTS.
Plymouth
Smarts Mtn. 3,240
Lyme
Squam L.
Ashland
Newfound L.
Mt. Cardigan 3,121
Bristol
Meredith
Ossipee L.
Center Ossipee
Ossipee

BELKNAP
Winnisquam L.
L. Winnipesaukee
Wolfeboro
Franklin
Laconia
Tilton
Belmont
Northfield

New London
Mt. Kearsarge 2,937
Sutton
Warner
Pittsfield
Farmington
Bradford
Contoocook
Henniker
MERRIMACK
Hopkinton
Concord ⊛
Pembroke
Allenstown
Suncook
Hooksett

SULLIVAN

Antrim
Hillsboro
Goffstown
Massabesic L.
GRENIER A.F.B.
Manchester
Derry

CHESHIRE
Keene
Marlborough
W. Swanzey
Troy
Mt. Monadnock 3,166
Jaffrey
Peterborough
Wilton
Milford
Greenville

HILLSBORO
ROCKINGHAM

Winchester
Winchendon
Townsend
Nashua
Hudson
Salem Depot
Salem
Lawrence
Dracut
Lowell

Greenfield

VERMONT

MAINE

Connecticut River
Ammonoosuc
Androscoggin
Saco
Pemigewasset
Merrimack River
Contoocook R.
Ashuelot R.
Black R.
West R.
Surry Mt. Res.

Kennebago L.
Flagstaff L.
Aziscoos L.
Rangeley L.
Mooselookmeguntic L.
Richardson Lakes
Umbagog L.
Norway
Kezar L.
Mechanic Falls
Lewiston
Glen
Bridgton
Long L.
Sebago L.
Gorham
Westbrook
Portland
Springvale
Sanford
Biddeford
Kennebunk
E. Rochester
Somersworth
Rochester
STRAFFORD
Dover
Salmon Falls
Durham
Great Bay
Newmarket
PEASE A.F.B.
Portsmouth
Kittery
Epping
Exeter
Hampton
Rye Beach
Isles of Shoals
Newington
Amesbury
Haverhill
Newburyport
Plaistow
Plum I.
Ipswich
Cape Ann Rockport
Gloucester

ATLANTIC OCEAN

N

45°
44°
43°

1
2
3
4

© C.S. HAMMOND & Co., Maplewood, N.J.

155

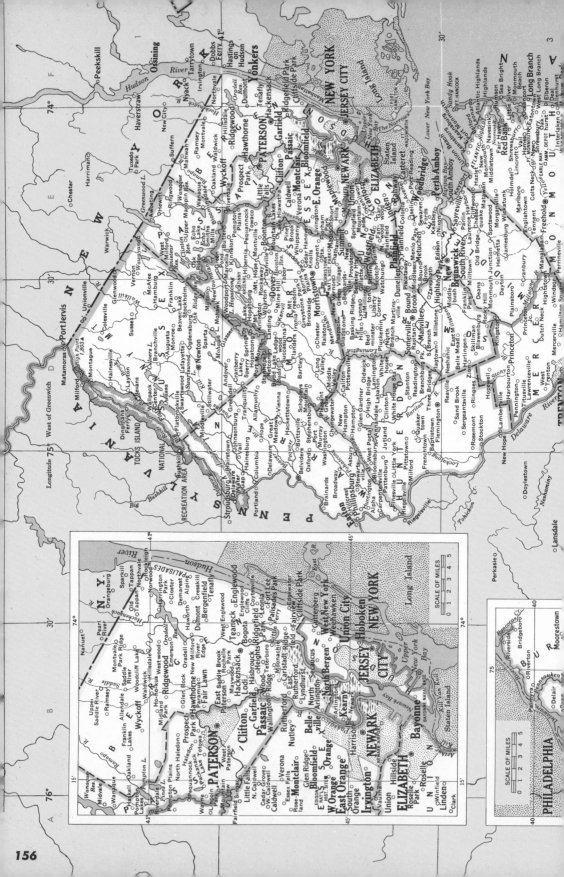

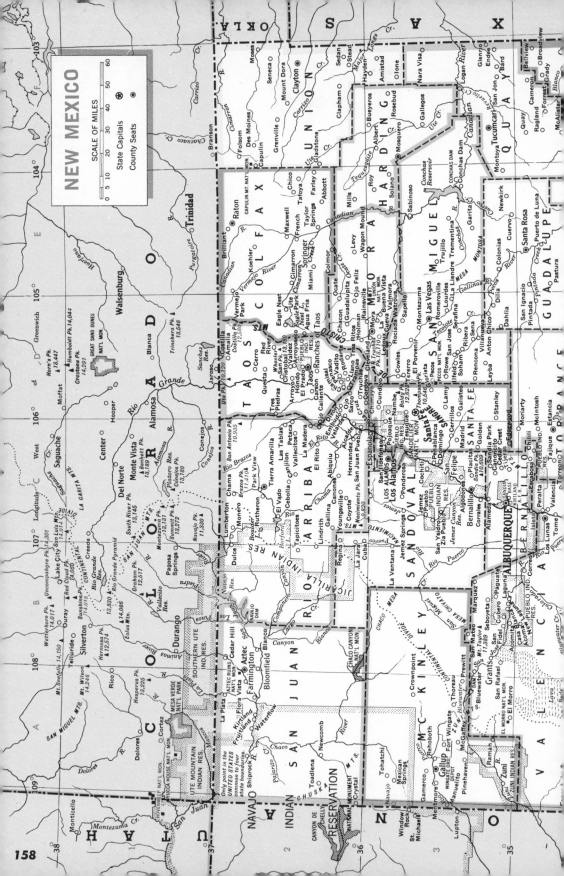

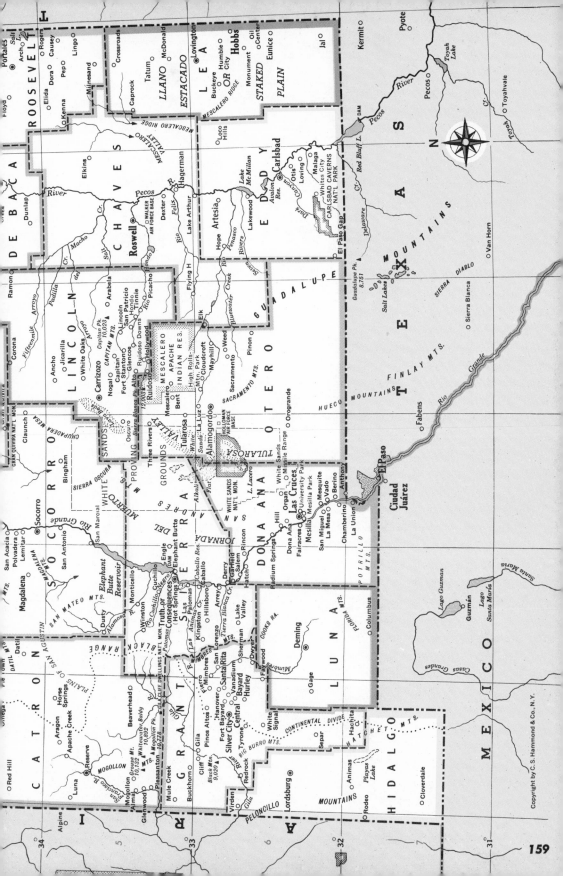

WESTERN PART OF
NORTH CAROLINA
Same scale as main map.

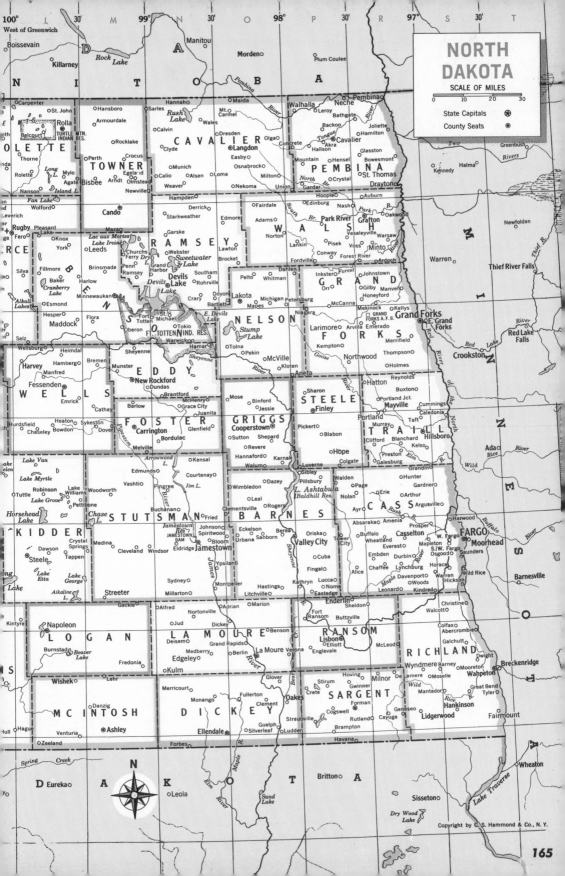

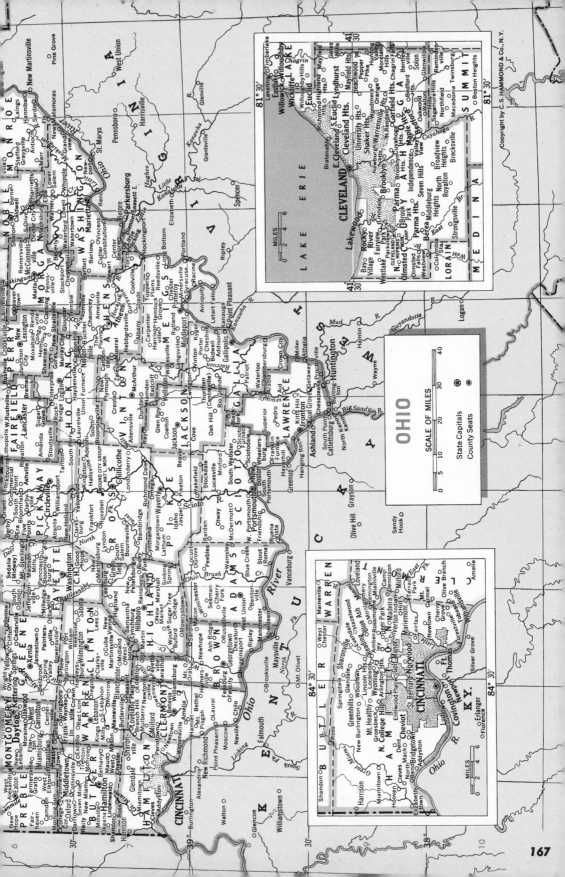

SCALE OF MILES
0 5 10   20   30   40

State Capitals ⊛
County Seats ⊙

OKLAHOMA

Copyright by C. S. Hammond & Co., N. Y.

169

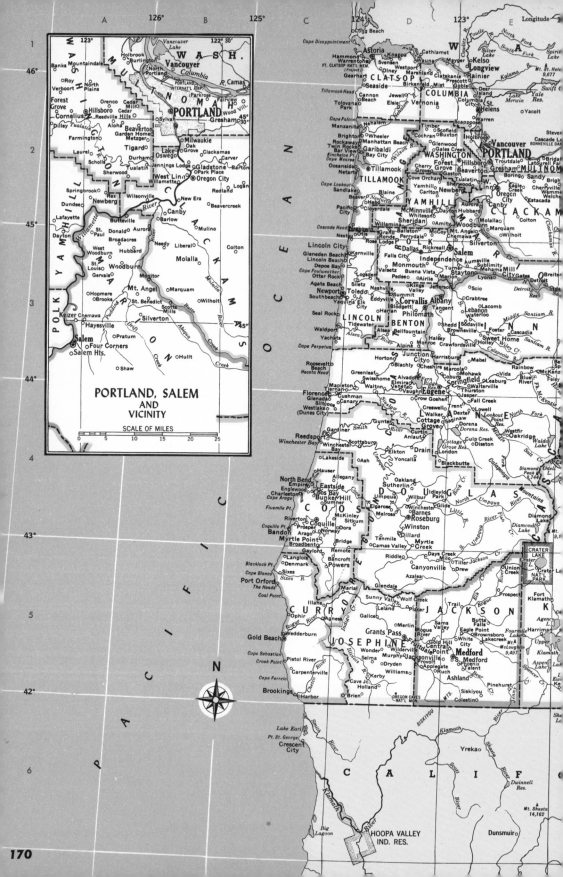

PORTLAND, SALEM
AND
VICINITY

SCALE OF MILES

0   5   10   15   20   25

170

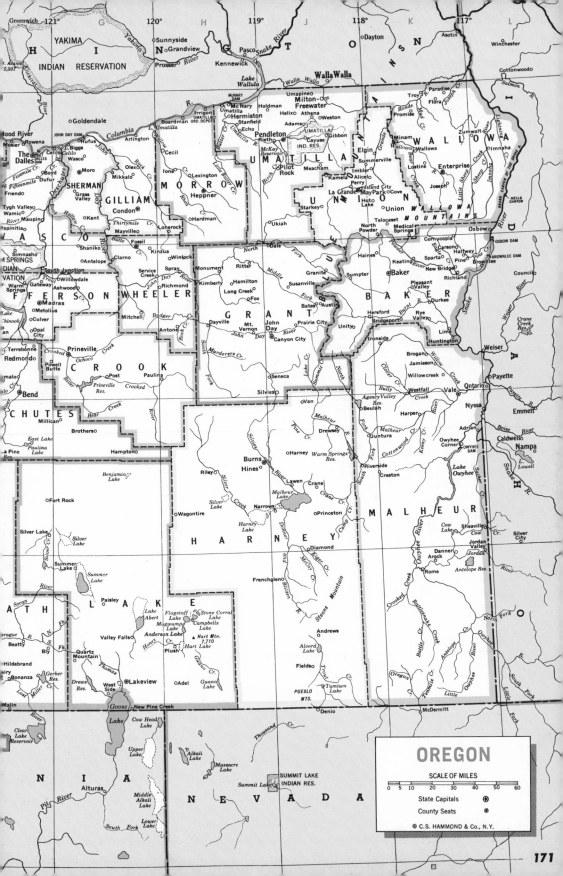

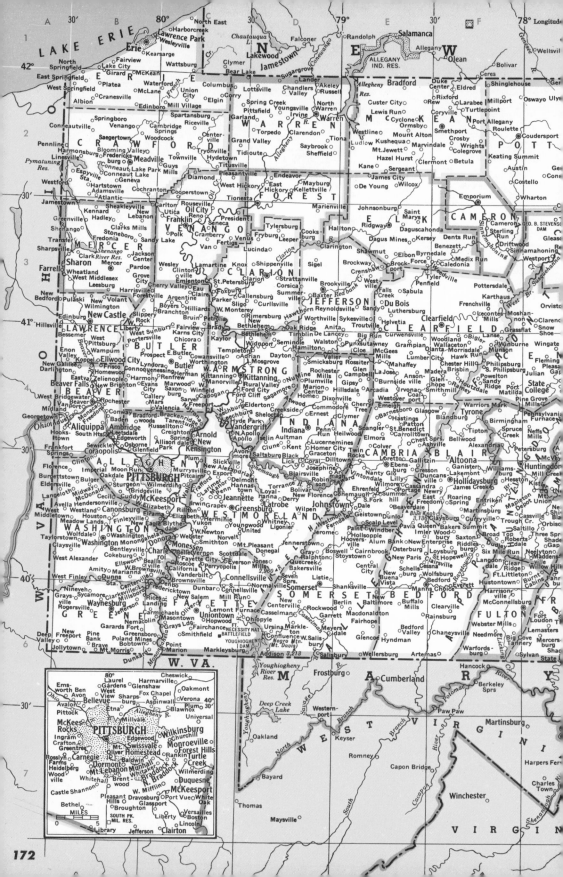

PENNSYLVANIA

SCALE OF MILES

0 5 10   20   30   40

⊛ State Capitals
⊙ County Seats
Canals

© C.S. Hammond & Co., N.Y.

173

SOUTH CAROLINA

SCALE OF MILES

0 5 10 20 30 40

⊛ State Capitals
⊙ County Seats
Canals

174

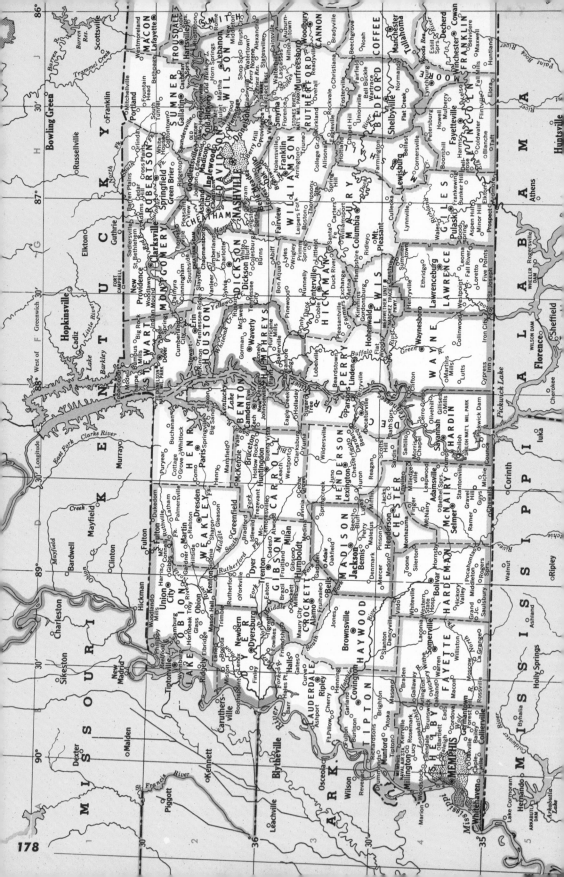

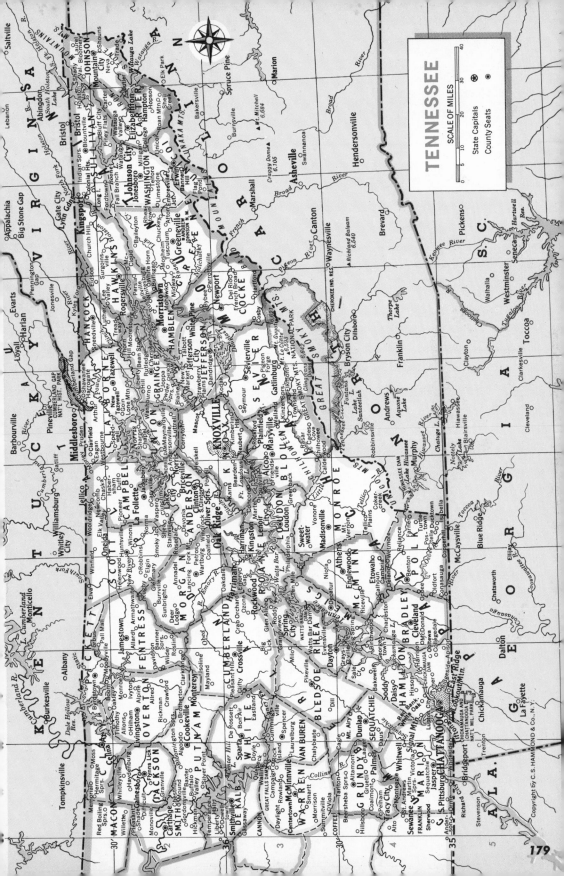

179

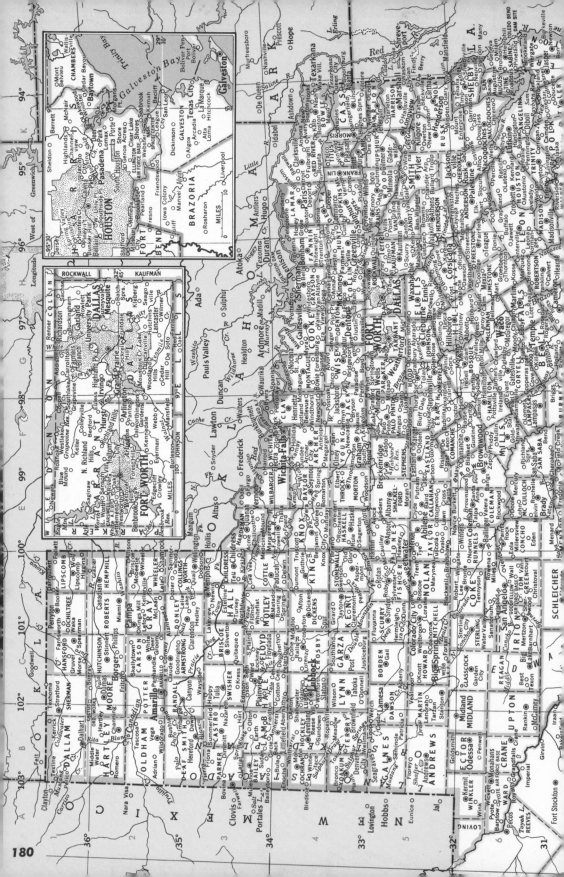

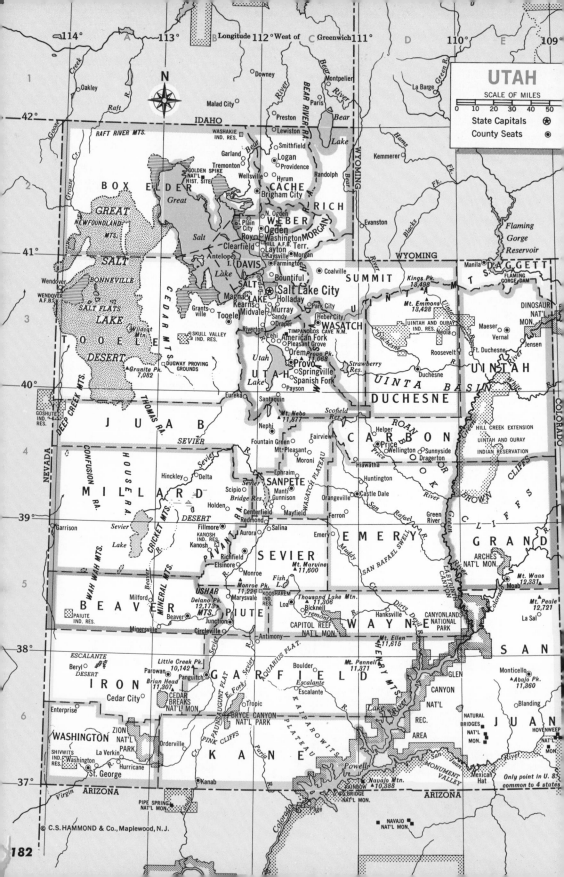

UTAH
SCALE OF MILES
0 10 20 30 40 50
State Capitals ✪
County Seats ◉

© C.S. Hammond & Co., Maplewood, N.J.

VERMONT

SCALE OF MILES

0   5   10   15   20   25

⊗ State Capitals
⊙ County Seats
   Canals

Copyright by C. S. Hammond & Co., N. Y.

183

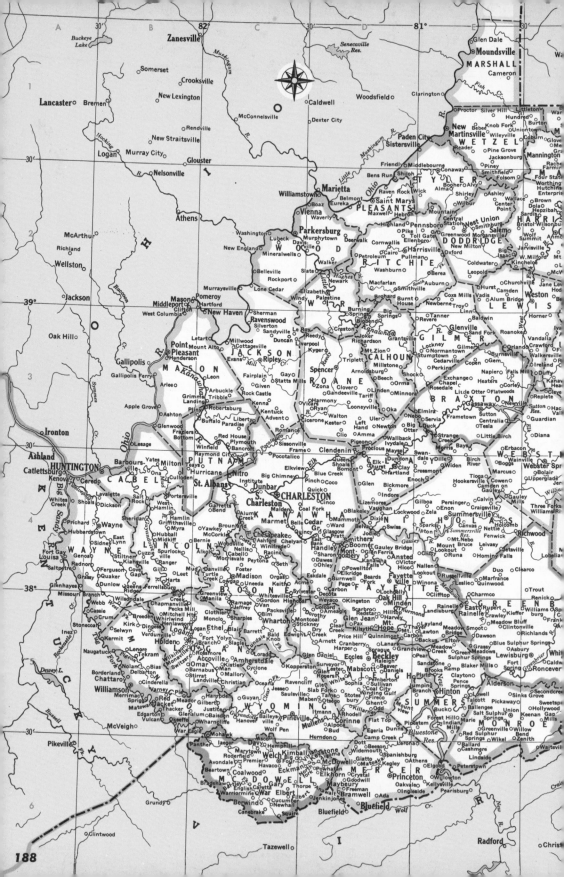

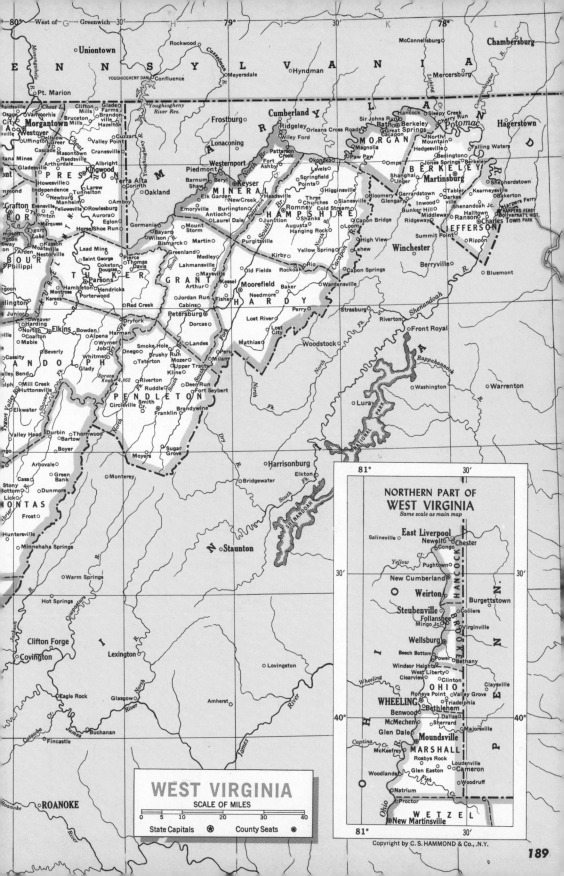

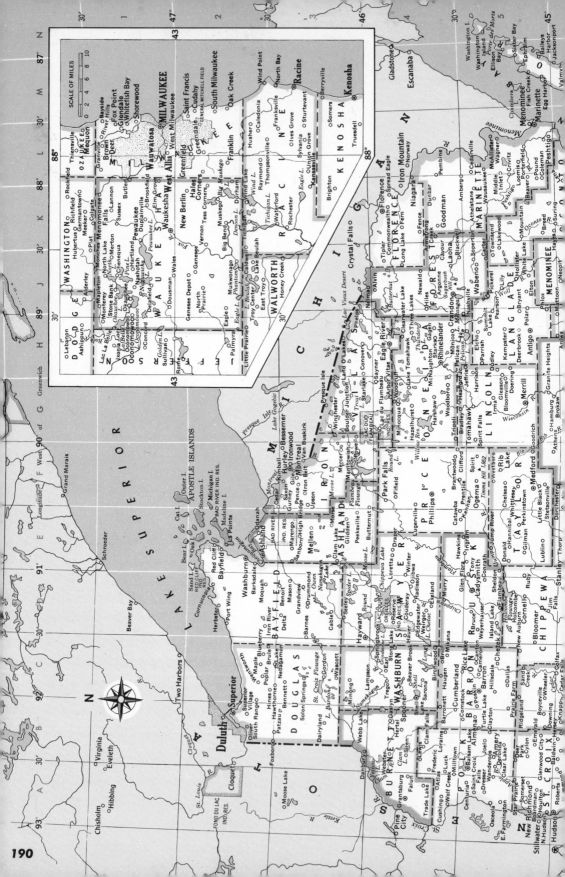

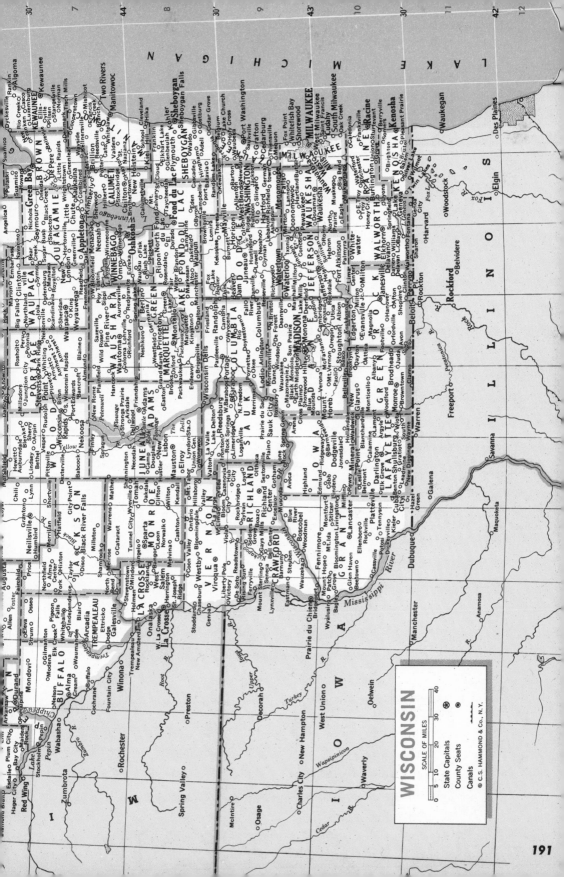

WISCONSIN

SCALE OF MILES

0 5 10 20 30 40

State Capitals ⊛
County Seats ⊙
Canals

© C. S. HAMMOND & CO., N.Y.

191

GLOSSARY OF GEOGRAPHICAL TERMS

A. = Arabic Camb. = Cambodian Ch. = Chinese Dan. = Danish Du. = Dutch
Finn. = Finnish Fr. = French Ger. = German Ice. = Icelandic It. = Italian
Jap. = Japanese Mong. = Mongol Nor. = Norwegian Per. = Persian
Port.=Portuguese Russ.=Russian Sp.=Spanish Sw.=Swedish Turk. =Turkish

Term	Language	Meaning
Å	Nor., Sw.	Stream
Abajo	Sp.	Lower
Ada, Adasi	Turk.	Island
Altiplano	Sp.	Plateau
Älv, Alf, Elf	Sw.	River
Arrecife	Sp.	Reef
Baai	Du.	Bay
Bahía	Sp.	Bay
Bahr	Arabic	Marsh, Lake, Sea, River
Baia	Port.	Bay
Baie	Fr.	Bay, Gulf
Bañados	Sp.	Marshes
Barra	Sp.	Reef
Belt	Ger.	Strait
Ben	Gaelic	Mountain
Berg	Ger., Du.	Mountain
Bir	Arabic	Well
Boca	Sp.	Gulf, Inlet
Bolshoi, Bolshaya	Russ.	Big
Bolsón	Sp.	Depression
Bong	Korean	Mountain
Bucht	Ger.	Bay
Bugt	Dan.	Bay
Bukhta	Russ.	Bay
Burnu, Burun	Turk.	Cape, Point
By	Dan., Nor., Sw.	Town
Cabo	Port., Sp.	Cape
Campos	Port.	Plains
Canal	Port., Sp.	Channel
Cap, Capo	Fr., It.	Cape
Catarátas	Sp.	Falls
Central, Centrale	Fr., It.	Middle
Cerrito, Cerro	Sp.	Hill
Ciénaga	Sp.	Swamp
Ciudad	Sp.	City
Col	Fr.	Pass
Cordillera	Sp.	Mt. Range
Côte	Fr.	Coast
Cuchilla	Sp.	Mt. Range
Dağ, Dagh	Turk.	Mountain
Dağlari	Turk.	Mt. Range
Dal	Nor., Sw.	Valley
Darya	Per.	Salt Lake
Dasht	Per.	Desert, Plain
Deniz, Denizi	Turk.	Sea, Lake
Desierto	Sp.	Desert
Eiland	Du.	Island
Elv	Dan., Nor.	River
Emi	Berber	Mountain
Erg	Arabic	Dune, Desert
Est, Este	Fr., Port., Sp.	East
Estrecho, Estreito	Sp., Port.	Strait
Étang	Fr.	Pond, Lagoon, Lake
Fjørd	Dan., Nor.	Fiord
Fleuve	Fr.	River
Gebel	Arabic	Mountain
Gebirge	Ger.	Mt. Range
Gobi	Mongol	Desert
Gol	Mongol, Turk.	Lake, Stream
Golf	Ger., Du.	Gulf
Golfe	Fr.	Gulf
Golfo	Sp., It., Port.	Gulf
Gölü	Turk.	Lake
Gora	Russ.	Mountain
Grand, Grande	Fr., Sp.	Big
Groot	Du.	Big
Gross	Ger.	Big
Grosso	It., Port.	Big
Guba	Russ.	Bay, Gulf
Gunto	Jap.	Archipelago
Gunung	Malay	Mountain
Higashi, Higasi	Jap.	East
Ho	Ch.	River
Hoek	Du.	Cape
Holm	Dan., Nor., Sw.	Island
Hu	Ch.	Lake
Hwang	Ch.	Yellow
Île	Fr.	Island
Insel	Ger.	Island
Irmak	Turk.	River
Isla	Sp.	Island
Isola	Sp.	Island
Jabal, Jebel	Arabic	Mountains
Järvi	Finn.	Lake
Jaure	Sw.	Lake
Jezira	Arabic	Island
Jima	Jap.	Island
Joki	Finn.	River
Kaap	Du.	Cape
Kabir, Kebir	Arabic	Big
Kanal	Russ., Ger.	Canal, Channel
Kap, Kapp	Nor., Sw., Ice.	Cape
Kawa	Jap.	River
Khrebet	Russ.	Mt. Range
Kiang	Ch.	River
Kita	Jap.	North
Klein	Du., Ger.	Small
Kô	Jap.	Lake
Ko	Thai.	Island
Koh	Camb., Khmer	Island
Köping	Sw.	Borough
Körfez, Körfezi	Turk.	Gulf
Kuh	Per.	Mountain

Kul	Sinkiang Turki	Lake
Kum	Turk.	Desert
Lac	Fr.	Lake
Lago	Port., Sp., It.	Lake
Lagôa	Port.	Lagoon
Laguna	Sp.	Lagoon
Lagune	Fr.	Lagoon
Llanos	Sp.	Plains
Mar	Sp., Port.	Sea
Mare	It.	Sea
Meer	Du.	Lake
Meer	Ger.	Sea
Mer	Fr.	Sea
Meseta	Sp.	Plateau
Minami	Jap.	Southern
Misaki	Jap.	Cape
Mittel	Ger.	Middle
Mont	Fr.	Mountain
Montagne	Fr.	Mountain
Montaña	Sp.	Mountains
Monte	Sp., It., Port.	Mountain
More	Russ.	Sea
Muong	Siamese	Town
Mys	Russ.	Cape
Nam	Burm., Lao	River
Nevado	Sp.	Snow covered peak
Nieder	Ger.	Lower
Nishi, Nisi	Jap.	West
Nizhni, Nizhnyaya	Russ.	Lower
Nor	Mong.	Lake
Nord	Fr., Ger.	North
Norte	Sp., It., Port.	North
Nos	Russ.	Cape
Novi, Novaya	Russ.	New
Nusa	Malay	Island
O	Jap.	Big
Ö	Nor., Sw	Island
Ober	Ger.	Upper
Occidental, Occidentale	Sp., It.	Western
Oeste	Port.	West
Oriental	Sp., Fr.	Eastern
Orientale	It.	Eastern
Ost	Ger.	East
Ostrov	Russ.	Island
Ouest	Fr.	West
öy	Nor.	Island
Ozero	Russ.	Lake
Pampa	Sp.	Plain
Paso	Sp.	Pass
Passo	It., Port.	Pass
Pequeño	Sp.	Small
Peski	Russ.	Desert
Petit	Fr.	Small
Pic	Fr.	Mountain
Pico	Port., Sp.	Mountain, Peak
Pik	Russ.	Peak
Pointe	Fr.	Point
Poluostrov	Russ.	Peninsula
Ponta	Port.	Point
Presa	Sp.	Reservoir
Proliv	Russ.	Strait
Pulou, Pulo	Malay	Island
Punta	Sp., It., Port.	Point
Ras	Arabic	Cape
Ría	Sp.	Estuary
Río	Sp.	River
Rivier, Rivière	Du., Fr.	River
Rud	Per.	River
Saki	Jap.	Cape
Salto	Sp., Port.	Falls
San	Ch., Jap., Korean	Hill
See	Ger.	Sea, Lake
Selvas	Sp., Port.	Forest
Serra	Port.	Mts.
Serranía	Sp.	Mts.
Severni, Servernaya	Russ.	North
Shan	Ch., Jap.	Hill, Mts.
Shima	Jap.	Island
Shoto	Jap.	Islands
Sierra	Sp.	Mountains
Sjö	Nor., Sw.	Lake, Sea
Spitze	Ger.	Mt. Peak
Sredni, Srednyaya	Russ.	Middle
Stad	Dan., Nor., Sw.	City
Stari, Staraya	Russ.	Old
Su	Turk.	River
Sud, Süd	Sp., Fr., Ger.	South
Sul	Port.	South
Sungei	Malay	River
Sur	Sp.	South
Tagh	Turk.	Mt. Range
Tal	Ger.	Valley
Tandjong, Tanjung	Malay	Cape, Point
Tso	Tibetan	Lake
Val	Fr.	Valley
Velho	Port.	Old
Verkhni	Russ.	Upper
Vesi	Finn.	Lake
Vishni, Vishnyaya	Russ.	High
Vostochni, Vostochnaya	Russ.	East, Eastern
Wadi	Arabic	Dry River
Wald	Ger.	Forest
Wan	Jap.	Bay
Yama	Jap.	Mountain
Yug, Yuzhni, Yuzhnaya	Russ.	South, Southern
Zaliv	Russ.	Bay, Gulf
Zapadni, Zapadnaya	Russ.	Western
Zee	Du.	Sea
Zemlya	Russ.	Land
Zuid	Du.	South

WORLD
STATISTICAL TABLES
and
DISTRIBUTION MAPS

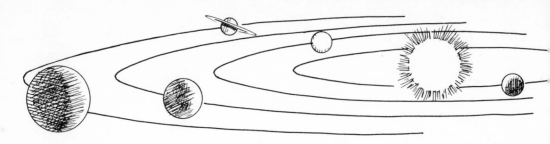

Elements of the Solar System

PLANETS	DISTANCE FROM SUN IN MILES		PERIOD OF REVOLUTION AROUND SUN IN DAYS	DIAMETER IN MILES	DENSITY (EARTH=1)
	MAXIMUM	MINIMUM			
Sun . . .	......	......	......	865,390	0.26
Mercury . .	43,404,000	28,599,000	87.87	3,009	0.68
Venus . . .	67,730,000	66,814,000	224.70	7,575	0.94
Earth . . .	94,560,000	91,446,000	365.26	7,927	1.00
Mars . . .	154,936,000	128,476,000	686.98	4,216	0.71
Jupiter . .	507,289,000	460,465,000	4,332.59	88,698	0.24
Saturn . .	936,637,000	837,655,000	10,759.20	75,060	0.12
Uranus . .	1,868,930,000	1,700,745,000	30,685.93	30,878	0.25
Neptune . .	2,820,610,000	2,773,510,000	60,187.64	27,700	0.41
Pluto . . .	4,585,000,000	2,753,000,000	90,470.23	3,600 approx.	0.7

Dimensions of the Earth

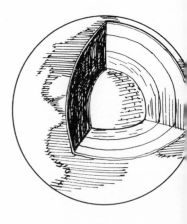

Superficial area	196,950,000	sq. miles
Land surface	57,510,000	" "
North America	8,500,000	" "
South America	6,814,000	" "
Europe	3,872,000	" "
Asia	16,990,000	" "
Africa	11,500,000	" "
Australia	2,974,581	" "
Water surface	139,440,000	" "
Atlantic Ocean	31,830,000	" "
Pacific Ocean	63,801,000	" "
Indian Ocean	28,356,000	" "
Arctic Ocean	5,440,000	" "
Equatorial circumference	24,902	miles
Meridional circumference	24,860	"
Equatorial diameter	7,926.677	"
Polar diameter	7,899.988	"
Equatorial radius	3,963.34	"
Polar radius	3,949.99	"
Volume of the Earth	260,000,000,000	cubic miles
Mass, or weight	6,592,000,000,000,000,000,000	tons
Mean distance from the Sun	92,897,416	miles

The Moon, the only satellite of the Earth, from which her mean distance is 238,857 miles, occupies an average period, in her revolution round the earth, of 29 days, 12 hours, 44 minutes, 3 seconds; her diameter is 2,160 miles, and her mean density 0.60.

Principal Lakes and Inland Seas

	AREA IN SQ. MILES		AREA IN SQ. MILES
Caspian Sea	163,800	Lake Bangweulu . . . . . Approx.	1,000
Lake Superior	31,820	Vättern	733
Lake Victoria	26,828	Dead Sea	405
Lake Aral	24,900	Lake Balaton	266
Lake Huron	23,010	Lake Geneva	225
Lake Michigan	22,400	Lake of Constance	208
Lake Tanganyika	12,700	Lough Neagh	153
Lake Baikal	12,150	Lake Garda	143
Great Bear Lake	12,000	Lake Neuchâtel	83
Great Slave Lake	11,170	Lake Maggiore	82
Lake Nyasa	11,000	Lough Corrib	71
Lake Erie	9,940	Lake Como	56
Lake Winnipeg	9,398	Lake of Lucerne	44.5
Lake Ontario	7,540	Lake of Zürich	34
Lake Ladoga	7,100		
Lake Balkhash	6,700		
Lake Chad	6,500		
Lake Onega	3,765		
Lake Titicaca	3,200		
Lake Nicaragua	3,100		
Lake Athabasca	3,058		
Reindeer Lake	2,444		
Issyk-Kul	2,276		
Vänern	2,149		
Lake Urmia	1,795		
Great Salt Lake	1,700		
Lake Albert	1,640		
Lake Van	1,453		
Lake Peipus	1,400		
Lake Tana	1,219		

Oceans and Seas of the World

	AREA IN SQ. MILES	GREATEST DEPTH IN FEET	VOLUME IN CUBIC MILES
Pacific Ocean	63,801,000	35,400	162,870,600
Atlantic Ocean	31,830,000	30,246	75,533,900
Indian Ocean	28,356,000	22,968	69,225,200
Arctic Ocean	5,440,000	17,850	4,029,400
Mediterranean Sea	1,145,000	15,197	1,019,400
Bering Sea	876,000	13,422	788,500
Caribbean Sea	750,000	23,748	2,298,400
Sea of Okhotsk	590,000	11,070	454,700
East China Sea	482,000	10,500	52,700
Hudson Bay	475,000	1,500	37,590
Japan Sea	389,000	13,242	383,200
North Sea	222,000	2,654	12,890
Red Sea	169,000	7,254	53,700
Black Sea	165,000	7,200	....
Baltic Sea	163,000	1,506	5,360

Longest Rivers of the World

	LENGTH IN MILES		LENGTH IN MILES		LENGTH IN MILES
Nile, Africa	4,149	Lena, U.S.S.R.	2,648	Danube, Europe	1,725
Amazon, S.A.	3,900	Mackenzie, Canada	2,635	Euphrates, Asia	1,700
Mississippi-Missouri, U.S.A.	3,710	Mekong, Asia	2,600	Indus, Asia	1,700
Yangtze, China	3,400	Niger, Africa	2,600	Brahmaputra, Asia	1,680
Ob-Irtysh, U.S.S.R.	3,200	Parana, S.A.	2,450	Syr-Dar'ya, U.S.S.R.	1,680
Congo, Africa	2,900	Yenisey, U.S.S.R.	2,364	Ganges, India	1,650
Amur, Asia	2,704	Murray-Darling, Australia	2,310	Orinoco, S.A.	1,600
Hwang (Yellow), China	2,700	Volga, U.S.S.R.	2,290	Zambezi, Africa	1,600
		Madeira, S.A.	2,000	Ural, US.S.R.	1,574
		Yukon, Alaska-Canada	1,979	Amu-Dar'ya, U.S.S.R.	1,550
		St. Lawrence, Canada-U.S.A.	1,900	Paraguay, S.A.	1,500
		Rio Grande, U.S.A.-Mexico	1,885	Arkansas, U.S.A.	1,450
		São Francisco, S.A.	1,800	Colorado, U.S.A.-Mexico	1,450
		Salween, Asia	1,750	Dnieper, U.S.S.R.	1,418
				Rio Negro, S.A.	1,400
				Orange, Africa	1,350
				Irrawaddy, Burma	1,325
				Ohio, U.S.A.	1,306
				Don, U.S.S.R.	1,222
				Columbia, U.S.A.-Canada	1,214
				Saskatchewan, Canada	1,205
				Tigris, Asia	1,150
				Snake, U.S.A.	1,038
				Red, Texas, U.S.A.	1,018
				Uruguay, S.A.	1,000
				Magdalena, Colombia	1,000
				Platte-N. Platte, U.S.A.	990
				Canadian, U.S.A.	906
				Tennessee, U.S.A.	862
				Dniester, U.S.S.R.	852
				Fraser, Canada	850
				Colorado, Texas, U.S.A.	840

Great Ship Canals

	LENGTH IN MILES	DEPTH IN FEET
Baltic-White Sea, U.S.S.R.	141	....
Suez, Egypt	100.76	34
Albert, Belgium	81	16.5
Moscow-Volga, U.S.S.R.	80	18
Kiel, Germany	61	37
Göta, Sweden	54	10
Panama, Canal Zone, U.S.A.	50.72	41
Houston, U.S.A.	50	36
Amsterdam-Rhine, Netherlands	45	41
Beaumont-Port Arthur, U.S.A.	40	32
Manchester, England	35.5	28
Chicago Sanitary and Ship, U.S.A.	30	22
Welland, Canada	27.6	25
Juliana, Netherlands	21	11.8
Chesapeake-Delaware, U.S.A.	19	27
Cape Cod, U.S.A.	13	25
Lake Washington, U.S.A.	8	30
Corinth, Greece	4	26.25
Sault Ste. Marie, U.S.A.	1.6	24.5
Sault Ste. Marie, Canada	1.4	18.25

Principal Mountains of the World

	FEET			FEET
Mt. Everest, Nepal-Tibet	29,028		Mt. Ararat, Turkey	16,945
Mt. Godwin Austen (K2), India	28,250		Ruwenzori, Africa	16,795
Kanchenjunga, Nepal-India	28,168		Cartensz, W. Irian	16,400
Dhaulagiri, Nepal	26,810		Klyuchevskaya Sopka, U.S.S.R.	15,912
Nunga Parbat, India	26,620		Mont Blanc, France	15,781
Annapurna, Nepal	26,504		Kazbek, US.S.R.	15,558
Nanda Devi, India	25,645		Monte Rosa, Italy-Switzerland	15,217
Mt. Kamet, India	25,447		Ras Dashan, Ethiopia	15,157
Gurla Mandhata, Tibet	25,355		Mt. Markham, Antarctica	15,100
Tirich Mir, Pakistan	25,263		Matterhorn, Switzerland	14,780
Minya Konka, China	24,900		Mt. Whitney, California	14,495
Mt. Communism, U.S.S.R.	24,590		Mt. Elbert, Colorado	14,431
Pobeda Peak, U.S.S.R.	24,406		Mt. Rainier, Washington	14,410
Muztagh Ata, China	24,388		Mt. Shasta, California	14,162
Chomo Lhari, India-Tibet	23,997		Pikes Peak, Colorado	14,110
Muztagh, China	23,890		Finsteraarhorn, Switzerland	14,026
Aconcagua, Argentina	22,834		Mauna Kea, Hawaii	13,796
Ojos del Salado, Argentina-Chile	22,539		Mauna Loa, Hawaii	13,680
Cerro Mercedario, Argentina	22,211		Jungfrau, Switzerland	13,667
Huascarán, Peru	22,205		Cameroon, Cameroon	13,350
Llullaillaco Volcano, Chile	22,057		Gran Paradiso, Italy	13,323
Tupungato, Chile-Argentina	21,489		Mt. Robson, British Columbia	12,972
Sajama Volcano, Bolivia	21,391		Grossglockner, Austria	12,461
Illampu, Bolivia	21,276		Fuji, Japan	12,389
Vilcanota, Peru	20,664		Mt. Cook, New Zealand	12,349
Chimborazo, Ecuador	20,561		Mulhacén, Spain	11,417
Mt. McKinley, Alaska	20,320		Mt. Etna, Italy	10,741
Mt. Logan, Yukon	19,850		Irazú, Costa Rica	10,525
Kilimanjaro, Tanzania	19,565		Lassen Peak, California	10,466
Cotopaxi, Ecuador	19,347		Mt. Kosciusko, Australia	7,316
El Misti, Peru	19,199		Mt. Mitchell, No. Carolina	6,684
Mt. Demavend, Iran	18,934			
Citlaltépetl, Mexico	18,700			
Mt. Elbrus, U.S.S.R.	18,481			
Mt. St. Elias, Alaska-Yukon	18,008			
Popocatépetl, Mexico	17,887			
Dikh-Tau, U.S.S.R.	17,085			
Mt. Kenya, Kenya	17,058			

Principal Islands of the World

	AREA IN SQ. MILES		AREA IN SQ. MILES		AREA IN SQ. MILES
Greenland	839,999	Prince of Wales	12,830	Tahiti	600
New Guinea	345,054	Vancouver	12,408	Oahu	589
Borneo	289,859	Sicily	9,926	Guadeloupe	583
Madagascar	241,094	Somerset	9,370	Ahvenanmaa (Åland Is.)	564
Baffin	183,810	Sardinia	9,301	Kauai	551
Sumatra	164,148	New Caledonia	7,201	Shetland Islands	550
Philippines	115,600	Fiji Islands	7,015	Rhodes	542
New Zealand: North and		New Hebrides	5,700	Caroline Islands	525
South Islands	103,934	Kuril Islands	5,700	Martinique	425
England-Scotland-Wales	88,745	Falkland Islands	4,618	Pemba	380
Honshu	87,426	Jamaica	4,411	Orkney Islands	376
Ellesmere	82,119	Bahama Islands	4,404	Madeira Islands	308
Victoria	81,930	Hawaii	4,021	Dominica	290
Celebes	72,986	Cape Breton	3,970	Tonga or Friendly	
Java	48,842	New Ireland	3,800	Islands	269
Cuba	42,857	Cyprus	3,572	Molokai	261
Newfoundland	42,734	Puerto Rico	3,421	St. Lucia	238
Luzon	40,420	Corsica	3,367	Corfu	229
Iceland	39,709	Crete	3,232	Bornholm	227
Mindanao	36,537	Galápagos Islands	3,042	Isle of Man	227
Sakhalin	35,400	Hebrides	3,000	Singapore	225
Novaya Zemlya	35,000	Canary Islands	2,894	Guam	212
Ireland	32,060	Wrangel	2,819	Isle Royale	209
Molucca Islands	30,168	Kerguélen	2,700	Virgin Islands	191
Hispaniola	29,843	Prince Edward	2,184	Curaçao	173
Hokkaido	29,600	Balearic Islands	1,936	Barbados	166
Tasmania	26,215	Trinidad and Tobago	1,864	Seychelles	155
Ceylon	25,332	Madura	1,752	St. Vincent	150
Timor	24,450	South Georgia	1,600	Isle of Wight	147
Svalbard (Spitsbergen)	24,294	Cape Verde Islands	1,557	Lanai	141
Banks	23,230	Long I., New York	1,401	Grenada	133
Devon	20,861	Socotra	1,400	Malta	122
Bismarck Arch.	19,660	Gotland	1,225	Tobago	116
Solomon Islands	18,670	Samoa	1,209	Martha's Vineyard	106
Tierra del Fuego	18,500	Isle of Pines	1,180	Channel Islands	75
Melville	16,369	Réunion	970	Nantucket	60
Southampton	15,700	Azores	890	St. Helena	47
New Britain	14,600	Fernando Po	785	Ascension	34
Taiwan (Formosa)	13,885	Tenerife	785	Hong Kong	29
Kyushu	13,770	Maui	728	Manhattan, New York	22
Hainan	13,000	Mauritius	720	Bermudas	21
		Zanzibar	640		

200

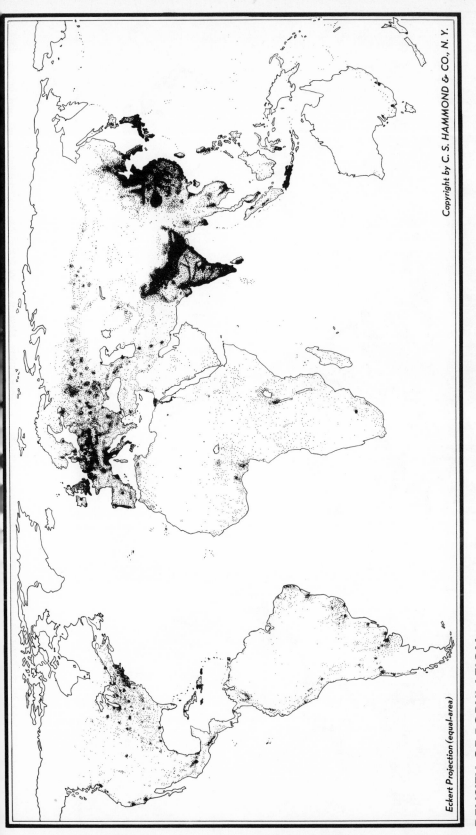

Eckert Projection (equal-area)

DENSITY OF POPULATION. One of the most outstanding facts of human geography is the extremely uneven distribution of people over the Earth. One-half of the Earth's surface has less than 3 people per square mile, while in the lowlands of India, China, Java and Japan rural density reaches the incredible congestion of 2000-3000 per square mile. Three-fourths of the Earth's population live in four relatively small areas; Northeastern United States, North-Central Europe, India and the Far East.

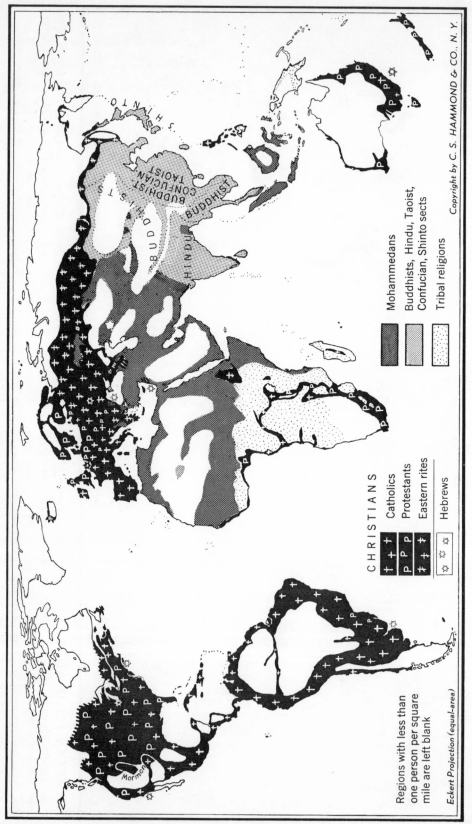

RELIGIONS. Most people of the Earth belong to four major religions: Christians, Mohammedans, Brahmans, Buddhists and derivatives. The Eastern rites of the Christians include the Greek Orthodox, Greek Catholic, Armenian, Syrian, Coptic and more minor churches. The lamaism of Tibet and Mongolia differs a great deal from Buddhism in Burma and Thailand. In the religion of China the teachings of Buddha, Confucius and Tao are mixed, while in Shinto a great deal of ancestor and emperor worship is added. About 11 million Hebrews live scattered over the globe, chiefly in cities and in the state of

Map legend:

CHRISTIANS
- ✝ ✝ ✝ Catholics
- P · P · P Protestants
- ✝ ✝ ✝ Eastern rites
- ✡ ✡ Hebrews

Mohammedans

Buddhists, Hindu, Taoist, Confucian, Shinto sects

Tribal religions

Regions with less than one person per square mile are left blank

Eckert Projection (equal-area)

Copyright by C. S. HAMMOND & CO., N. Y.

Map labels: SHINTO · BUDDHIST CONFUCIAN TAOIST · BUDDHISTS · HINDU · Mormon

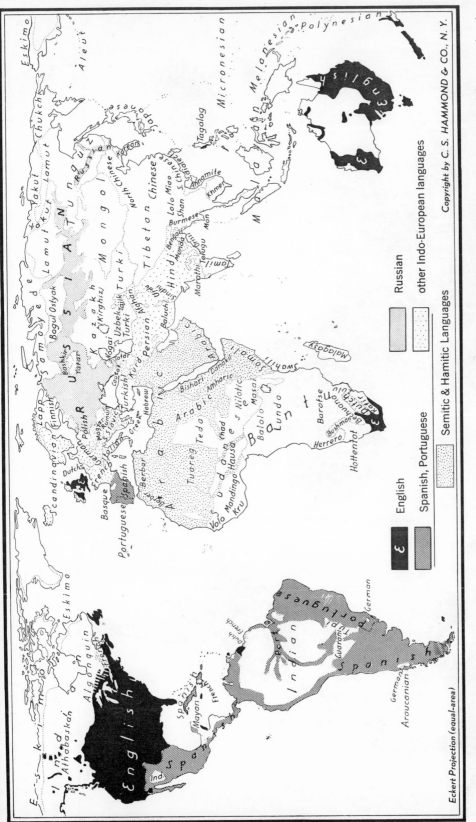

LANGUAGES. *Several hundred different languages are spoken in the World, and in many places two or more languages are spoken, sometimes by the same people. The map above shows the dominant languages in each* locality. *English, French, Spanish, Russian, Arabic and Swahili are spoken by many people as a second language for commerce or travel.*

Eckert Projection (equal-area)

Copyright by C. S. HAMMOND & CO., N. Y.

English

Spanish, Portuguese

Semitic & Hamitic Languages

Russian

other Indo-European languages

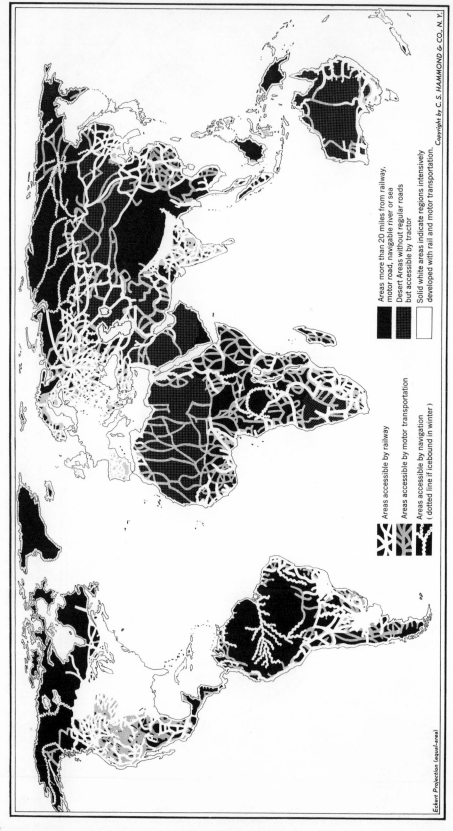

Eckert Projection (equal-area)

Copyright by C. S. HAMMOND & CO., N. Y.

Areas accessible by railway

Areas accessible by motor transportation

Areas accessible by navigation (dotted line if icebound in winter)

Areas more than 20 miles from railway, motor road, navigable river or sea

Desert Areas without regular roads but accessible by tractor

Solid white areas indicate regions intensively developed with rail and motor transportation.

ACCESSIBILITY. *Many regions in the world are far from railways, roads, navigable rivers or the seas. Their economic development is retarded because their products can be brought to the world's markets only at great expense. Such areas are in the tundra (alpine), the boreal forest and in the equatorial rain forest regions. Desert areas, if not too mountainous, can be crossed by tractors. The largest inaccessible area is in Tibet, on account of high mountains, the alpine climate and isolationist attitude of the people. Airplane transportation is helping to bring these inaccessible areas into the orbit of civilization.*

204

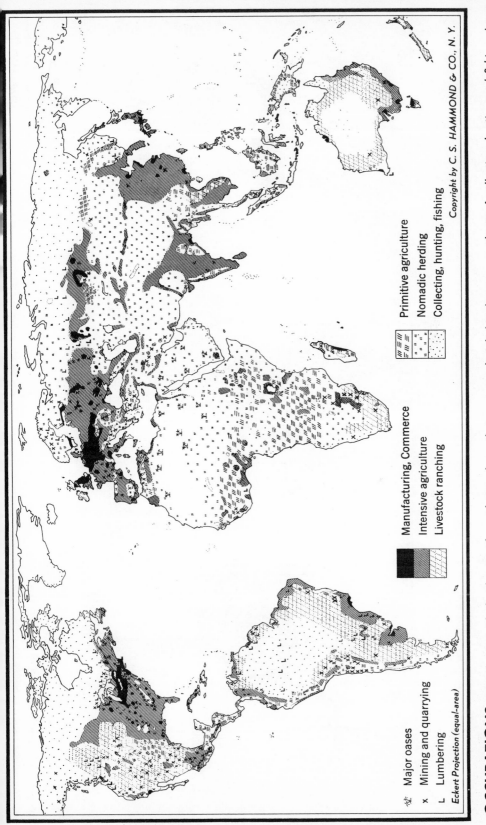

OCCUPATIONS. Correlation with the density of population shows that the most densely populated areas fall into the regions of manufacturing and intensive farming. All other economies require considerable space. The most sparsely inhabited areas are those of collecting, hunting and fishing. Areas with practically no habitation are left blank.

Manufacturing, Commerce
Intensive agriculture
Livestock ranching

Primitive agriculture
Nomadic herding
Collecting, hunting, fishing

⚒ Major oases
× Mining and quarrying
L Lumbering

Eckert Projection (equal-area)

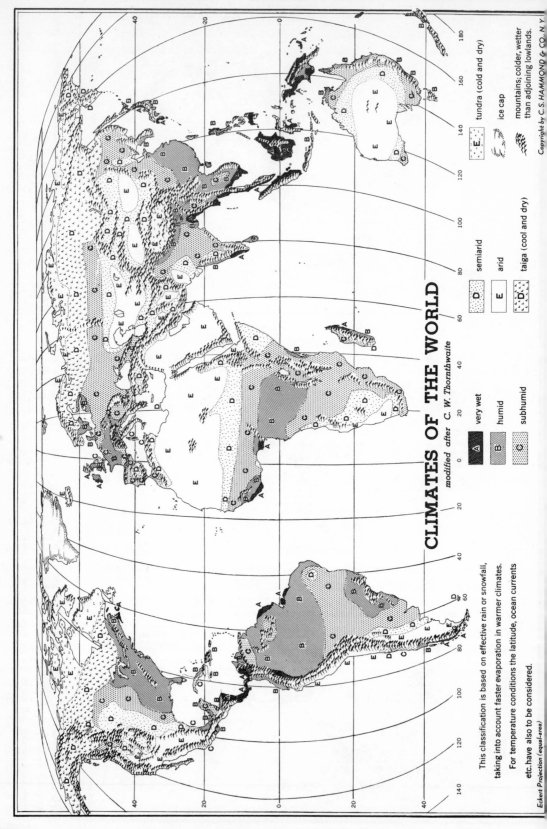

CLIMATES OF THE WORLD

modified after C. W. Thornthwaite

This classification is based on effective rain or snowfall,
taking into account faster evaporation in warmer climates.
For temperature conditions the latitude, ocean currents
etc. have also to be considered.

very wet **A**

humid **B**

subhumid **C**

semiarid **D**

arid **E**

taiga (cool and dry) **D**

tundra (cold and dry) **E**

ice cap

mountains; colder, wetter
than adjoining lowlands.

Copyright by C. S. HAMMOND & CO., N. Y.

Eckert Projection (equal-area)

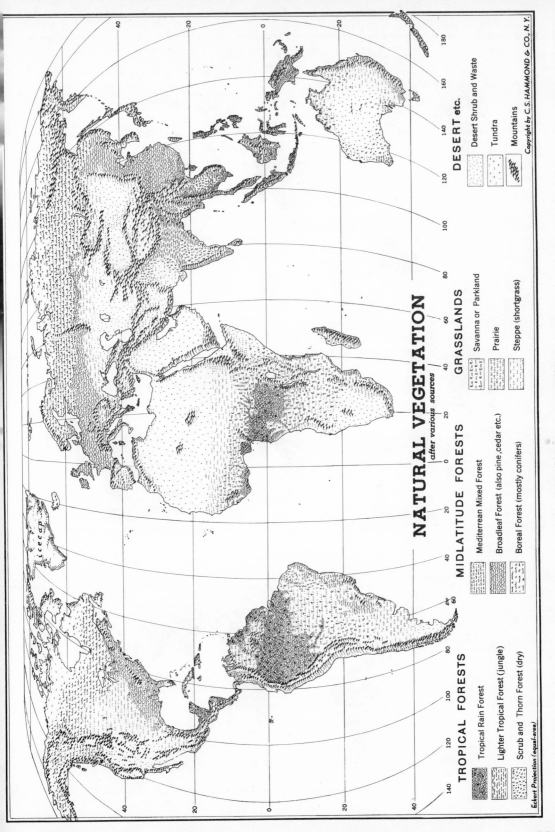

NATURAL VEGETATION
after various sources

TROPICAL FORESTS
- Tropical Rain Forest
- Lighter Tropical Forest (jungle)
- Scrub and Thorn Forest (dry)

MIDLATITUDE FORESTS
- Mediterrean Mixed Forest
- Broadleaf Forest (also pine, cedar etc.)
- Boreal Forest (mostly conifers)

GRASSLANDS
- Savanna or Parkland
- Prairie
- Steppe (shortgrass)

DESERT etc.
- Desert Shrub and Waste
- Tundra
- Mountains

Copyright by C. S. HAMMOND & CO., N.Y.

Eckert Projection (equal-area)

207

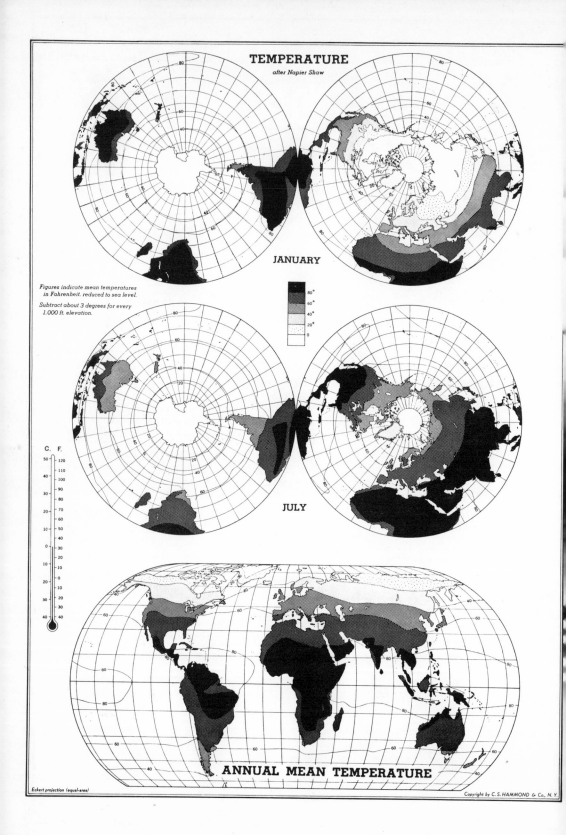

TEMPERATURE

after Napier Shaw

JANUARY

Figures indicate mean temperatures in Fahrenheit, reduced to sea level.

Subtract about 3 degrees for every 1,000 ft. elevation.

JULY

ANNUAL MEAN TEMPERATURE

Eckert projection (equal-area)

Copyright by C. S. HAMMOND & Co., N. Y.

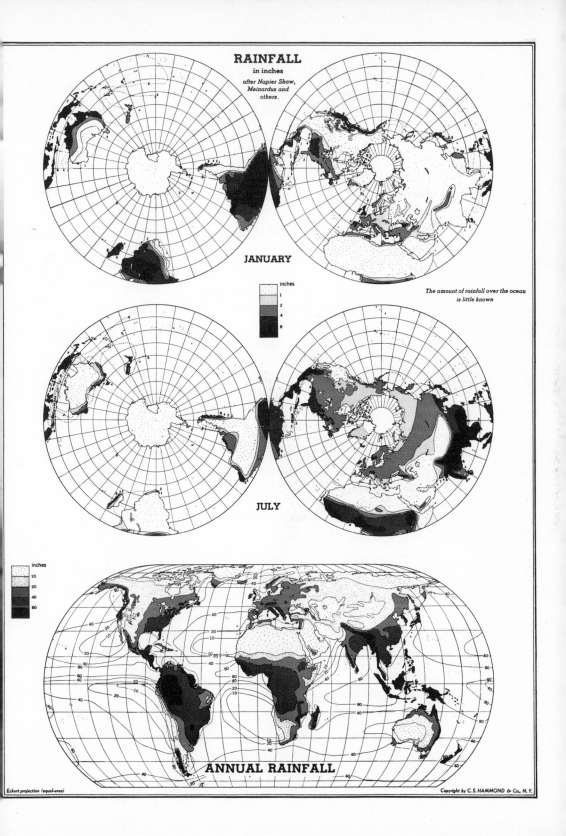

RAINFALL
in inches
*after Napier Shaw,
Meinardus and
others.*

JANUARY

inches
1
2
4
8

*The amount of rainfall over the ocean
is little known*

JULY

inches
10
20
40
80

ANNUAL RAINFALL

Eckert projection (equal-area)

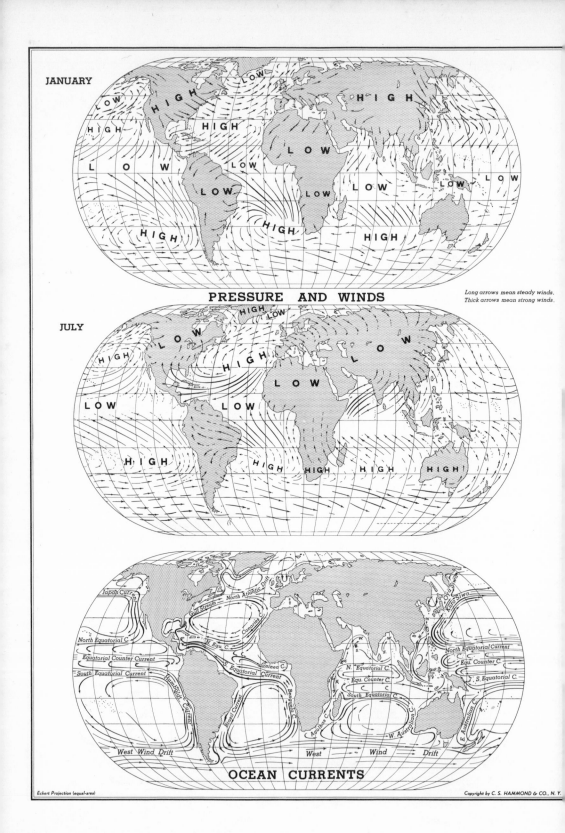

JANUARY

PRESSURE AND WINDS

Long arrows mean steady winds.
Thick arrows mean strong winds.

JULY

OCEAN CURRENTS

Eckert Projection (equal-area)

Copyright by C. S. HAMMOND & CO., N. Y.

Illustrated

Social and Economic Tables
of the World

N.Y. State Dep't of Commerce

The headline events of the last half-century have made the average person acutely curious of the vast world beyond his country's borders. This new national concern for the external world and its problems is one of the hopeful signs pointing to a better future for mankind. However, no matter how well-intentioned our concern for international relations may be, it is of no value unless it is grounded on an intelligent appreciation of the great diversity of social, economic and political forms extant throughout the globe.

On the following pages the editors have presented information on the world's nations, products, peoples and governments arranged in easily-found tabular form. This arrangement by tables makes comparison between political units a simpler task. These data, used with the maps in this atlas, complete the story of the nations of the world.

Social and Economic Tables

POLITICAL DIVISION	GOVERNMENT	MONETARY UNIT	LANGUAGE	RELIGION
AFARS & ISSAS, TERR. OF THE	French overseas territory with a governor and elected executive council and territorial assembly.	Djibouti franc	Hamitic languages Arabic; French	Mohammedan
AFGHANISTAN	Constitutional monarchy, with an appointed prime minister, cabinet, and a partly elected bicameral legislature.	afghani	Pushtu (Afghan) Farsi (Persian)	Mohammedan
ALBANIA	Soviet-type republic with a head of state, cabinet and unicameral legislature, actually controlled by the Communist party politburo.	lek	Albanian (Gheg, Tosk)	Moslem Orthodox Roman Catholic
ALGERIA	Republic at present under a president, council of ministers, and a revolutionary council.	Algerian dinar	Arabic French Berber	Mohammedan Roman Catholic Judaist
AMERICAN SAMOA	U.S. territory with a governor and a bicameral legislature.	American dollar	English Samoan	Protestant
ANDORRA	A republic under the joint suzerainty of the French State and the Bishop of Urgel, with a council general of 24 elective members. Executive authority is vested in the First Syndic.	French franc and Spanish peseta	Catalan	Roman Catholic
ANGOLA	Portuguese overseas province with a governor-general.	Portuguese escudo	Bantu languages Portuguese	Tribal religions Roman Catholic
ANTIGUA	Self-governing state associated with the United Kingdom, with a governor, chief minister, and executive and legislative councils.	B.W.I. dollar	English	Protestant
ARGENTINA	A republic with a president, vice-president, appointive cabinet, elective senate and house of deputies.	Argentine peso	Spanish	Roman Catholic
AUSTRALIA	Independent British Commonwealth member with a governor-general, prime minister, cabinet, and a bicameral parliament, composed of a senate and a house of commons.	Australian dollar	English	Protestant Roman Catholic
AUSTRIA	Republic with a president, chancellor and vice-chancellor, cabinet of ministers, and two-house assembly.	schilling	German	Roman Catholic
BAHAMA ISLANDS	A Counstitutional self-governing British State, with a governor, prime minister, a cabinet and a bicameral legislature.	Bahaman dollar	English	Roman Catholic Protestant
BAHREIN	British protected sheikhdom, advised by a political agent.	Bahrein dinar	Arabic	Mohammedan
BARBADOS	Independent British Commonwealth member, with a governor, prime minister, privy council and a bicameral legislature.	B.W.I. dollar	English	Protestant

of the World

MAJOR PRODUCTS

Boats, sheep; hides; salt.

Wheat, barley, millet, corn, rice, lentils, vegetables, fruits, nuts, cotton, tobacco, fat-tailed sheep (karakul), camels, wool, skins; sheepskin, textiles, leather, carpets; gold, iron, lapis lazuli, coal, copper, lead, silver, natural gas, talc.

Corn, tobacco, wheat, oats, barley, rye, rice, cotton, sugar beets, olives, fruit; cattle, sheep; fish; wool, hides; dairy products, furs; bitumen, salt, lignite, petroleum, copper, iron, chromite, flour, olive oil, cheese, cement, timber.

Wheat, barley, oats, corn, grapes, olives, tobacco, dates, figs, citrus fruits, vegetables, potatoes; sheep, goats, cattle, mules, horses, pigs, camels; hides and skins; fish; timber; iron, phosphates, zinc, natural gas, salt, lead, petroleum; wine, olive oil, carpets, cotton weaving, tobacco products, wool, cork, cement, chemicals, machinery.

Copra, taro, breadfruit, yams, bananas, arrowroot, pineapples, oranges; mats.

Tobacco, potatoes, rye, barley; sheep, cattle; lumber; dairy products.

ALGERIA: A native letter writer in the streets of Constantine, the country's third largest city.

TWA—Trans World Airlines

Coffee, corn, sugar, palm products, cotton, wheat, sisal, wax, tobacco; iron ore, diamonds; fish products, sugar.

Sugar cane, cotton, tropical fruits and vegetables, fish; barite; sugar, rum.

Wheat, corn, oats, barley, linseed, rye, grapes, cotton, sugar cane, potatoes, tobacco, vegetables; yerba maté; cattle, sheep; quebracho, lumber; petroleum, zinc, manganese, gold, lead, iron, tungsten; oils, wines, hides, wool, meats, textiles, metal products, vehicles and machinery, chemicals, wood and paper products, leather, flour, dairy products, cement.

Wheat, oats, rice, barley, fruits, vegetables, sugar; sheep, cattle; gold, coal, copper, iron, lead, silver, tin, zinc; timber, iron and steel, wool, textiles, electrical and radio equipment, appliances, drugs, chemicals, paints, optical instruments, agricultural implements, machinery, clothing, leather, furniture, airplanes, engines, ships, processed fruit and vegetables, dairy products, building materials, confectionery, automobiles.

Rye, wheat, oats, barley, corn, potatoes, sugar beets, hops, grapes, flax, hemp, tobacco; iron, copper, lead, magnesite, graphite, coal, aluminum, petroleum, lignite, salt; timber; pulp, poultry and livestock; steel, machinery, machine tools, chemicals, textiles, paper, processed foods, leather.

Tomatoes, pineapples, okra, vegetables, citrus fruits, bananas, sisal; crawfish, shells; lumber; salt; handcraft products, cement, pulpwood.

Pearl fishing, petroleum, boat building, fishing; reed mats, dates, lucerne; donkeys; textiles, building materials.

Sugar cane, cotton; flying fish; manjak (asphalt); sugar, molasses, rum, edible oil, margarine.

AUSTRALIA: The country's first oil field at Moonie, Queensland, is in a sheep herding region.

Australian Government

Social and Economic Tables

POLITICAL DIVISION	GOVERNMENT	MONETARY UNIT	LANGUAGE	RELIGION
BELGIUM	Constitutional, hereditary monarchy. King appoints a cabinet of ministers. Parliament consists of a senate and chamber of deputies.	Belgian franc	French (Walloon) and Flemish	Roman Catholic
BERMUDA	Constitutional British colony with a governor, executive and legislative councils, and an elected house of assembly.	Bermuda pound	English	Protestant
BOLIVIA	Constitutional republic, with a president, cabinet and bicameral legislature.	Bolivian peso	Spanish Indian languages	Roman Catholic
BOTSWANA	Constitutional republic, with a president, a unicameral legislature and an advisory House of Chiefs.	South African rand	Tswana; English Afrikaans Bushman	Tribal religions Protestant
BRAZIL	Federal republic with a president, vice-president, appointive secretaries of state and a bicameral legislature.	cruzeiro	Portuguese	Roman Catholic
BRITISH HONDURAS	Self-governing British colony with governor, prime minister, cabinet and bicameral legislature.	Br. Honduras dollar	English Spanish	Protestant Roman Catholic
BRUNEI	British protected sultanate, with a chief minister, privy council, and executive and legislative councils.	Malayan dollar	Malay English	Mohammedan
BULGARIA	Soviet-type republic with a one-house legislature, which elects a presidium whose president is the nominal chief of state. Actual power is Communist politburo.	lev	Bulgarian	Eastern Orthodox Mohammedan
BURMA, UNION OF	One party republic, at present under a revolutionary council of ministers.	kyat	Burmese Karen Shan	Buddhist Tribal religions
BURUNDI	Republic with a president, a cabinet, and a revolutionary committee.	Burundi franc	Kirundi French	Tribal religions Roman Catholic
CAMBODIA	Constitutional monarchy, with a head of state, prime minister, and a national assembly.	riel	Khmer Lao French	Buddhist
CAMEROON	One party federal state of the French Community, with a president, cabinet, and unicameral legislature.	CFA franc	Sudanese and Bantu languages French; English	Tribal religions Mohammedan Christian
CANADA	Independent British Commonwealth member, with a governor-general, prime minister, cabinet, and a bicameral parliament, composed of a senate and a house of commons.	Canadian dollar	English French	Protestant Roman Catholic
CAPE VERDE ISLANDS	Portuguese overseas province, ruled by a governor.	Portuguese escudo	Portuguese	Roman Catholic

of the World

MAJOR PRODUCTS

Wheat, rye, oats, barley, potatoes, sugar beets, flax, tobacco, vegetables, fruit, hops, hemp, bulbs, livestock, fish; coal, iron, zinc, lead, copper, tin, silver; coke, steel, machinery, textiles, lace, glass, chemicals, uranium refining, sugar, margarine, cheese, vinegar, alcohol, beer, matches, paper, foods, beverages, wool, cut diamonds, dairy products.

Lily bulbs, onions, bananas, cabbage, tomatoes, beans; coral; fish; perfume, pharmaceuticals.

Potatoes, corn, wheat, rice, sugar, fruits, vanilla, rubber, quinine; tin, zinc, lead, copper, silver, antimony, tungsten, gold, sulphur, petroleum; cattle; textiles, flour, cement, tobacco products, hides, beer, earthenware.

Kaffir, cotton, peanuts, beans, fruit, wheat and wheatmeal; cattle, sheep, goats, pigs; hides, gold, asbestos, manganese; meat products.

Coffee, corn, rice, cotton, cacao, sugar cane, cassava, beans, carnauba wax, medicinal plants, tropical fruits, balata, tobacco, fibers, castor oil; livestock; nuts; iron, manganese, gold, zirconium, diamonds, mica, bauxite, quartz, beryllium, chrome, tungsten, silver; foods, textiles, chemicals, pharmaceuticals, metallurgical products, paper and wood products, hides, vegetable oils, machinery.

Rice, maize, beans, bananas, coconuts, citrus fruits, sugar cane; mahogany, chicle, pine, cedar; fish; rum, food products.

Rice, sago, rubber, jelutong, cutch, sugar cane, tapioca, bananas, pineapples; timber; domestic birds, buffalo, pigs, cattle; petroleum, natural gas; boat building, cloth, brass and silverware.

Wheat, corn, barley, oats, rye, tobacco, fruit, cotton, sugar beets, potatoes; livestock, silkworm cocoons; fish; coal, salt, bauxite, copper, iron, lead, manganese, silver, zinc, kaolin; tobacco products, attar of roses, sugar, flour, textiles, leather goods, shoes, lead concentrates, wines and spirits.

Rice, sesame, peanuts, corn, cotton, millet, tobacco, sugar, beans, fruit, vegetables, pulses, rubber; teak wood, lumber; cattle, buffalo, pigs; petroleum, silver, lead, zinc, tin, copper, tungsten, rubies, sapphires, amber, jade, nickel, gold, cobalt, salt; textiles, hides, matches, lacquer ware.

Agricultural products, coffee, tea, cotton; cattle; hides.

Rice, tobacco, kapok, cotton, pepper, corn, sugar, rubber; timber; cattle; fish; silk, cotton, textiles, pottery, rush mats; precious stones, phosphates, petroleum.

Cocoa, palm kernels, bananas, caoutchouc, coconuts, coffee, cacao, palm oil; timber; cattle, sheep, pigs, horses, asses; aluminum; rubber, tobacco, cotton products.

Wheat, oats, barley, flax, rye, potatoes, turnips, vegetables, sugar beets, tobacco, fruits, dairy products, livestock; fish; forestry products; furs; gold, copper, nickel, zinc, lead, silver, platinum, iron ore, titanium, cobalt, radium, uranium, petroleum, natural gas, coal, asbestos, salt, gypsum, quartz, sulphur, cement, clay; hydro-electric power; foods, beverages, transportation equipment, iron and steel products, aluminum, metal products, pulp, paper and wood products, textiles, electrical apparatus, chemicals.

Coffee, castor beans, corn, fruit, tobacco; goats, oxen, pigs, asses; hides, skins; preserved fish, salt, lime, sugar.

BELGIUM: The Grand' Place in Brussels, with its flower market surrounded by Gothic and Renaissance architecture.

Belgian Gov't Info. Ctr.

BRAZIL: Baling cotton for export by rail and sea in the state of São Paulo.

Pan American Union

Social and Economic Tables

POLITICAL DIVISION	GOVERNMENT	MONETARY UNIT	LANGUAGE	RELIGION
CENTRAL AFRICAN REPUBLIC	One party republic of the French Community, at present under a president and a revolutionary council.	CFA franc	Sudanese and Bantu languages French	Mohammedan Tribal religions Roman Catholic
CEYLON	Independent member of the British Commonwealth ruled by a governor-general, a prime minister, a cabinet and a bicameral legislature.	Celanese rupee	Sinhala Tamil English	Buddhist Hindu Christian Mohammedan
CHAD	One party republic of the French Community, with a president and a national assembly.	CFA franc	Bantu and Sudanese languages Arabic, French	Tribal religions Mohammedan Roman Catholic
CHILE	Republic with a president, cabinet and a bicameral legislature.	Chilean escudo	Spanish	Roman Catholic
CHINA: MAINLAND (COMMUNIST)	In theory, governmental power resides in the National People's Congress and the State Council. In practice, power resides in the Communist Party's Central Committee.	Chinese (People's Bank) dollar (yuan)	Chinese Mongol Turki	Confucianist Buddhist Taoist Mohammedan
CHINA: TAIWAN (NATIONALIST)	A republic with a popularly elected National Assembly, which elects the president and vice-president. Legislative powers reside with the Legislative Yuan.	New Taiwan dollar (yuan)	Chinese	Confucianist Buddhist Taoist Christian Tribal religions
COLOMBIA	A centralized federal republic with a president, vice-president, appointive cabinet, elective senate and house of representatives.	Colombian peso	Spanish	Roman Catholic
COMORO ISLANDS	Internally self-governing French overseas territory, with a high commissioner, council, and an elected chamber of deputies.	CFA franc	Arabic French	Mohammedan
CONGO, REPUBLIC OF	Republic of the French Community, with a president and a legislative assembly.	CFA franc	Sudanese and Bantu languages French	Mohammedan Tribal religions Roman Catholic
CONGO, DEM. REPUBLIC OF THE	Constitutional republic, with a president, prime minister and a national assembly.	zaire	Bantu languages French	Tribal religions Roman Catholic
COOK ISLANDS	Internally self-governing state in association with New Zealand with a commissioner, prime minister and a cabinet.	New Zealand dollar	Polynesian dialects English	Protestant
COSTA RICA	Republic with president, cabinet and one-house legislature.	colón	Spanish	Roman Catholic
CUBA	Nominal republic with a president and appointed cabinet, dictatorial powers being held by the prime minister.	Cuban peso	Spanish	Roman Catholic

of the World

MAJOR PRODUCTS

Coffee, cotton, sisal, groundnuts, millet, sorghum; timber; gold, diamonds; rubber; palm products, beeswax.

Tea, coconuts, rubber, rice, millet, tobacco, cacao, cinnamon, citronella, cloves, fruits, palmyra, fish; cattle, buffalo, goats, swine; graphite, plumbago, mica, ilmenite, monazite; salt, pearls, zircon, copra, plywood, leather, shoes, glass, steel, acetic acid, ceramics, quinine, strychnine, shark-liver oil, coconut oil, textiles.

Millet, sesame, groundnuts, vegetables; livestock, hides; ivory, ostrich feathers; cotton, dates.

Wheat, potatoes, oats, rice, barley, corn, kidney beans, lentils, fruits; fish; livestock; copper, silver, nitrates, iodine, iron ore, gold, manganese, coal; foods, textiles, leather, wood products, cement, chemicals and pharmaceuticals, wines and beer, wool, iron and steel, petroleum, paper and pulp.

Rice, wheat, potatoes, corn, barley, millet, kaoliang, soybeans, cotton, tea, sugar cane, tobacco, peanuts, peas, beans, opium, tung, silk; pigs, cattle, sheep, goats, buffalo, donkeys, horses, mules, poultry; timber; fish; iron, coal, tungsten, tin, antimony, mercury, copper, lead, zinc, silver, bauxite, manganese, gold, petroleum, molybdenum; foodstuffs, textiles, chemicals, machinery, metal work, metallurgical products, cement, clothing, embroideries, ceramics.

Rice, tea, sugar, sweet potatoes, ramie, jute, turmeric, pineapples, bananas, camphor; pigs; buffalo, cattle, goats, horses; canned foods, metal products, machinery, textiles, wood products.

Coffee, sugar cane, corn, rice, potatoes, cotton, bananas, cacao, wheat, tobacco, cinchona; cattle; rubber, fibers; petroleum, gold, silver, platinum, emeralds, salt; textiles, beer, sugar, cement, flour, tobacco products, iron and steel.

Sugar cane, vanilla, rice, sweet potatoes, yams, copra, sisal, cloves, cacao, perfume plants; rum distilling.

Palm oil and kernels, hardwoods, kola nuts, coffee, cocoa, copal, rubber, tobacco; lead, gold, petroleum, diamonds, livestock; rice.

Palm oil and kernels, cotton, coffee, oil cakes, tea, cocoa, rice, groundnuts; rubber, manioc, fibers; cattle, sheep, goats; copper, coal, silver, tin, diamonds, gold, cobalt, radium, uranium, tantulum, zinc, manganese.

Citrus fruits, coconuts, copra, tomatoes, arrowroot, pineapples, breadfruit, taro, kumaras, plantains, yams; mother-of-pearl.

Coffee, bananas, cocoa, abacá, sugar cane, maize, rice, tobacco; cattle; tuna; gold, silver; cigars and cigarettes, textiles, furniture and woodwork, sugar, electric goods.

Sugar cane, tobacco, coffee, pineapples, citrus fruits, bananas, henequen; cattle; timber; fish; chromite, iron, manganese, copper, nickel; sugar, textiles, alcohol, molasses, chemicals, tobacco products, electrical goods, clothing, steel.

CHILE: Bathers and cabanas on the Pacific sands of Las Salinas, a popular beach at Viña del Mar.

COLOMBIA: One of the country's principal products, coffee, drying under the tropical sun.

Social and Economic Tables

POLITICAL DIVISION	GOVERNMENT	MONETARY UNIT	LANGUAGE	RELIGION
CYPRUS	British Commonwealth republic, with a president (Greek), vice-president (Turkish), cabinet, and Greek and Turkish communal chambers.	Cypriot pound	Greek Turkish	Greek Orthodox Mohammedan
CZECHOSLOVAKIA	Soviet-type republic with a president, a National Assembly and a Slovak National Council, with actual power residing in the Communist party presidium.	koruna (crown)	Czech and Slovak	Roman Catholic
DAHOMEY	Republic of the French Community, at present under a president and a revolutionary committee.	CFA franc	Sudanese languages French	Tribal religions Mohammedan
DENMARK	Constitutional, hereditary monarchy with a two-house, elective legislature and an appointive council of ministers.	krone (crown)	Danish	Protestant
DOMINICAN REPUBLIC	Nominal republic with a bicameral legislature.	Dominican peso	Spanish	Roman Catholic
ECUADOR	Constitutional republic with a bicameral legislature and a president.	sucre	Spanish Indian languages (Quechua, etc.)	Roman Catholic
EGYPT	See: United Arab Republic.			
EL SALVADOR	Republic with a president, cabinet, and unicameral legislature.	colón	Spanish	Roman Catholic
ENGLAND AND WALES	Integral part of the United Kingdom, with executive power nominally residing in the Crown, but actually exercised by the prime minister, cabinet and bicameral parliament, composed of a house of lords and a house of commons.	pound sterling	English and Welsh (Celtic)	Protestant
EQUATORIAL GUINEA	Former Spanish overseas provinces. Independent republic established in 1968.	Spanish peseta	Bantu languages Spanish	Tribal religions Roman Catholic
ETHIOPIA	Constitutional monarchy with an emperor, a council of ministers and a bicameral legislature.	Ethiopian dollar	Amharic Hamitic languages English; French	Coptic Christian Mohammedan
FALKLAND ISLANDS	British colony with a governor and an executive and a legislative council.	pound sterling	English	Protestant Roman Catholic
FIJI	Partly self-governing British colony with a governor, chief minister and cabinet; Fijian Administration is advised by a council of chiefs.	Fiji pound (dollar-1969)	English Fijian Hindustani Chinese	Protestant Roman Catholic Hindu Moslem
FINLAND	A republic with a president, a one-house elective diet and appointive council of state.	markka (mark)	Finnish and Swedish	Protestant

of the World

MAJOR PRODUCTS

Wheat, barley, oats, grapes, raisins, olives, potatoes, carobs, cotton, tobacco, hemp, flax, citrus fruits, beans, corn, melons; sponges, fish; sheep, goats, cattle, pigs; copper and iron pyrites, asbestos, chromite, gypsum, copper concentrates; tobacco products, buttons, wines, false teeth, lace, gum, boots and shoes, dried fruits, cheese.

Wheat, rye, barley, oats, corn, hops, sugar beets, grapes, potatoes; poultry, livestock; timber; coal, lignite, iron, graphite, garnets, silver, copper, lead, salt, manganese, zinc; beer, spirits, malt, metals, munitions, machinery, iron and steel, porcelain, shoes, textiles, wood products, pulp and paper, sugar, leather, foods, chemicals, rubber products.

Palm products, tobacco, groundnuts, cotton, corn, copra, coffee, castor oil, kapok, millet; gold, diamonds, bauxite, iron ore.

Barley, oats, rye, wheat, potatoes, sugar beets; livestock, fish; clay; ships and transportation equipment, butter, bacon, eggs, cheese, milk, footwear, textiles, machines, chemicals, tobacco products, metal goods, leather goods, beverages; stone, earthenware, glassware, electrical goods.

Sugar cane, cacao, coffee, tobacco, bananas, rice, corn; cattle; lumber; gold, bauxite, starch, alcohol, molasses, chocolate, sugar, meats, cigars, cigarettes, leather.

Rice, cacao, coffee, bananas, rubber, kapok, cotton, nuts, cinchona; livestock; gold, petroleum, silver, salt, balsa wood; textiles, toquilla (panama) hats, buttons, sugar, flour, shoes, chemicals, pharmaceuticals, cement, soap, candles.

Coffee, cotton, corn, tobacco, henequen, sugar cane, rice; fish, livestock; balsa and other woods, gold, silver; cotton textiles, bags, sugar, pharmaceuticals.

Potatoes, turnips, beets, oats, wheat, barley, rye, hay, beans, peas, cabbage, vetches, hops, fruits; sheep, cattle, pigs, horses, poultry; fish; coal, coke, gas, iron, copper, lead, nickel, tin, clay; dairy products, wool, cotton and linen textiles; electrical goods, vehicles, steel, scientific instruments, cutlery, foods and beverages, tobacco products, clothing and shoes, chemicals, pottery, china, machinery, locomotives, carpets, knitwear, lace, pharmaceuticals.

Cocoa, coffee, bananas, palm oil and kernels, copra; cabinet woods.

Coffee, teff, barley, durra, wheat, cotton, oil seeds, sugar cane; cattle, sheep, goats, horses, mules; hides, skins; wax, gold, rocksalt.

Forage crops, sheep; wool, skins, tallow, whale oil, whale-meat meal.

Sugar cane, coconuts, rice, fruits, cotton, rubber, oil seeds, root vegetables, groundnuts, pulses, corn, tobacco; cattle, pigs; tuna, bêche-de-mer, trochus shell; gold, silver; sugar, copra, coconut oil, soap, biscuits, molasses, butter, ghee, candlenut oil.

Hay, potatoes, wheat, oats, barley, rye, sugar beets; cattle, horses, sheep, pigs, poultry, reindeer; wood and timber; fish; copper; lumber, plywood, furniture, pulp and paper, cardboard, textiles, butter, cheese, eggs, flour, leather, chemicals, china and glass, foodstuffs, machinery, ships.

DENMARK: Amalienborg Palace in Copenhagen, the king's residence, and the statue of King Frederik V.
Danish Nat'l Travel Office

FRANCE: Fresh fruits and vegetables occupy part of Les Halles, the central market of Paris, near the right bank of the Seine.
TWA–Trans World Airlines

Social and Economic Tables

POLITICAL DIVISION	GOVERNMENT	MONETARY UNIT	LANGUAGE	RELIGION
FRANCE	A republic with a president, a two-house elective parliament and an appointive council of ministers.	franc	French	Roman Catholic
FRENCH GUIANA	Overseas department of France governed by a prefect, with an elective council-general.	French franc	French	Roman Catholic
FRENCH POLYNESIA	Overseas territory of France, with a governor, government council, and an elected territorial assembly.	CFP franc	Polynesian dialects French	Protestant Roman Catholic
GABON	Equatorial African republic within the French Community with a president and a national assembly.	CFA franc	Bantu languages French	Tribal religions Roman Catholic
GAMBIA	Republic of the British Commonwealth, with a prime minister and a unicameral legislature.	Gambian pound	Sudanese languages English	Mohammedan Tribal religions Protestant
GERMANY	Country is divided between two governments — a democratic **Federal Republic of Germany** in the west and a Soviet-dominated **German "Democratic" Republic** in the east. **Federal Republic** has an elected federal diet and council who jointly elect the president. **German "Democratic" Republic** has a communist-controlled legislative branch which selects the president, cabinet and prime minister.	East German and West German Deutsch mark	German	Protestant Roman Catholic
GHANA	Republic of the British Commonwealth, at present under a military council.	cedi	Sudanese languages English	Mohammedan Tribal religions Protestant
GIBRALTAR	Partly self-governing British colony, with a governor, cabinet, and executive and legislative councils.	pound sterling	English and Spanish	Roman Catholic
GILBERT AND ELLICE ISLS.	British colony with a commissioner, governing council and house of representatives.	Australian dollar	English Gilbertese Samoan	Protestant Roman Catholic
GREAT BRITAIN	See: England and Wales, Northern Ireland, Scotland.			
GREECE	A constitutional hereditary monarchy with a prime minister, cabinet of ministers and an elective assembly, presently ruled by a junta.	drachma	Greek	Greek Orthodox
GREENLAND	Integral part of the Danish kingdom, with representation in Parliament and a provincial council.	Danish krone	Danish and Greenlandic	Protestant
GUADELOUPE	Overseas department of France with a prefect and elective general council.	French franc	French French Patois	Roman Catholic
GUAM	U.S. territory with a governor, advisory staff, and an elected, unicameral legislature.	American dollar	English Chamorro Spanish	Roman Catholic
GUATEMALA	Republic with a president, cabinet and one-house legislature.	quetzal	Spanish	Roman Catholic

of the World

MAJOR PRODUCTS

Sugar beets, potatoes, wheat, oats, barley, rye; corn, turnips, fruits, nuts, grapes, buckwheat; cattle, sheep, pigs, horses; fish; coal, iron ore, lignite, salt, bauxite, pyrites, potash salts, sulphur, natural gas, iron and steel, chemicals; silk, cotton, rayon, wool and linen, textiles; clothing, lace, perfumes and cosmetics, automobiles, machinery, dairy products, beet sugar, wines, porcelain, aluminum, foods, leather, lumber, spirits.

Rice, cacao, bananas, sugar cane, corn, cassava, woods; gold; hides, rosewood essence, shoes, rum, fish glue.

Coconuts, tropical fruits, vanilla, sugar cane, coffee, bamboo, pearls; phosphates; mother-of-pearl, sugar, rum, copra.

Tropical woods; gold, manganese, petroleum, natural gas, uranium; fish; cocoa; rubber, coffee, kapok, waxes, kola nuts; manioc, sweet potatoes, corn, plantains.

Groundnuts, rice, palm kernels; hides and skins; fish; beeswax.

Wheat, rye, barley, oats, potatoes, sugar beets, fruits, hops; pigs, cattle, poultry, horses; fish; forest products; coal, lignite, iron, copper, potash, sulphur, salt, uranium, lead, zinc, fluorspar, gypsum, vanadium, aluminum; automobiles, steel, cement, diesel oil, gasoline, cotton yarn, woolen yarn, rayon fiber, beet sugar, beer, wines, optical instruments, sulphuric acid, sodium bicarbonate, chemicals, machinery, electrical equipment, aircraft.

Cocoa, palm oil and kernels, sorghum, millet, corn, yams, cassava, groundnuts, cotton; timber; gold, diamonds, manganese, bauxite, silver; cocoa products.

Fish for export and processing of commodities for local consumption.

Coconuts, copra, phosphate of lime; pearl shell, fish; hats, mats.

Wheat, barley, corn, oats, rye, tobacco, currants, citrus fruits, olives, figs, grapes, cottonseed, sesame seed; sheep, goats, cattle, pigs, horses, mules; fish; iron ore, sulphur, emery, magnesite, zinc, lead, lignite, marble, silver, bauxite; textiles, olive oil, foods, wines, chemicals, leather, wood and paper, metal products, machinery.

Grass for fodder; cod and other fish; sheep, furs; cryolite; processed fish, hides.

Sugar cane, bananas, coffee, cocoa, vanilla, cassava; fish; alcohol, rum.

Coconut products, corn, taro, bananas, citrus fruits, mangoes, papayas, breadfruit, sweet potatoes, cocoa, cassava, sugar cane, pineapples; cattle, pigs, poultry, buffalo.

Coffee, bananas, sugar cane, rubber, cotton, wheat, corn, rice, chicle, cacao, abacá, cattle; mahogany, and dye woods; essential oils; gold; textiles, chemicals, drugs, wood and leather goods.

GREECE: An "evzone," one of the uniquely, uniformed guards at the Royal Palace in Athens.

J. Walter Thompson

GUATEMALA: Removing the nuts from the pods at a cacao "finca," or plantation, is the first stage of processing chocolate.

I.I.A.A.

Social and Economic Tables

POLITICAL DIVISION	GOVERNMENT	MONETARY UNIT	LANGUAGE	RELIGION
GUINEA	One party republic with a president, cabinet, and national assembly.	Guinea franc	Sudanese languages French	Tribal religions Mohammedan
GUYANA	Independent member of the British Commonwealth, with prime minister, cabinet, and unicameral legislature.	Guyana dollar	English	Protestant
HAITI	Republic with a president, cabinet, and a unicameral legislature.	gourde	Creole, French	Roman Catholic
HONDURAS	Republic with a president, council of ministers and a one-house legislature.	lempira	Spanish	Roman Catholic
HONG KONG	British colony ruled by a governor assisted by executive and legislative councils.	Hong Kong ● dollar	Chinese English	Confucianist Buddhist Christian
HUNGARY	Soviet-type republic with a president and council selected by the national assembly. Actual power in hands of politburo, highest organ of Communist party.	forint	Hungarian	Catholic Protestant
ICELAND	A republic with a president, an elective, two-house legislature and an appointive cabinet of ministers.	króna (crown)	Icelandic	Protestant
IFNI	Overseas province of Spain, ruled by a governor.	Spanish peseta	Berber Arabic Spanish	Mohammedan
INDIA	An independent republic within the British Commonwealth with a president, cabinet and a bicameral legislature.	Indian rupee	Hindi; English Assamese, Bengali, Gujarati, Kannada, Kashmiri, Malayalam, Marathi, Oriya, Punjabi, Sanskrit, Tamil, Teluga, Urdu; Bhutia, Lepcha	Hindu Mohammedan Buddhist Animist Christian Sikh Jain Parsi Lamaist
INDONESIA	Nominal republic headed by a military cabinet, with a "people's consultative congress."	rupiah	Indonesian (Malay, Javanese, etc.)	Mohammedan Christian Hindu Buddhist Tribal religions
IRAN	Constitutional monarchy governed by a shah, prime minister, cabinet and a bicameral legislature.	rial	Persian Arabic Kurdish	Mohammedan Zoroastrian Parsi
IRAQ	Republic with a president, prime minister, cabinet, and unicameral legislature, actually controlled by a revolutionary council.	Iraqi dinar	Arabic Turkish Kurdish	Mohammedan Christian
IRELAND	A republic with a president, premier and an elective, two-house parliament.	Irish pound	Irish (Gaelic) English	Roman Catholic Protestant

of the World

MAJOR PRODUCTS

Rice, groundnuts, palm oil and nuts, wax, honey, bananas, indigo, kola, orange products, coffee; cattle, sheep, goats; hides and skins; bauxite, iron ore, diamonds.

Sugar cane, rice, coconuts, coffee, citrus fruits, cacao; balata, rubber, green heart and other timber; livestock; bauxite, diamonds, gold; textiles, milled rice, beer and rum, lime rum and oil, sugar, woods, molasses, charcoal, matches.

Coffee, sugar, fig bananas, sisal, cotton, rice, cocoa, log-wood; bauxite, copper; molasses, sisal products.

Bananas, coffee, coconuts, tobacco, cotton, grapefruit, rice, henequen; mahogany; cattle; gold, silver.

Rice, sugar, ginger; fish; poultry, pigs; kaolin, lead, iron, wolfram, granite, silver, cement; shipbuilding; enameled hollow ware, textiles, wood and plastic products, jewelry.

Wheat, corn, rye, barley, oats, potatoes, sugar beets, tobacco, grapes and other fruits, peppers, hemp, flax; pigs, cattle, sheep, horses, poultry; fish; coal, lignite, petroleum, natural gas, iron ore, bauxite, manganese; flour, sugar, distilling, brewing, iron and steel, wines, textiles, paprika, chemicals, leather, metal products, wood and paper products.

Hay, potatoes, turnips, hothouse fruits and vegetables; sheep, poultry, horses, cattle; fish; dairy products, meats, animal and vegetable oils, hides, skins, leather, clothing, textiles, frozen fish, herring oil, herring meal.

Barley, alfalfa, corn, tomatoes, argan oil, wheat; fish.

Rice, wheat, legumes, groundnuts, oilseeds, tea, tobacco, jute, cotton, rubber, coffee, sugar cane, barley, millet, corn; cattle, goats, buffalo, sheep, pigs; fish; coal, manganese, gold, petroleum, salt, mica, iron, copper, chromite, ilmenite, diamonds, silver, bauxite; textiles, shawls, carpets, jute manufactures, wood-carving and metal work, leather, chem-icals, shipbuilding, petroleum refining, sugar refining, cotton ginning, iron and steel mills, glass, soap, matches.

Rice, sugar cane, rubber, palm oil, tobacco, corn, coconuts, copra, spices, sweet potatoes, groundnuts, tea, beans, cotton, kapok, coffee, cinchona, cocoa, pepper, fruits, vegetables; cattle, buffalo; tin, coal, petroleum, bauxite, nickel, copper, manganese; rubber goods, chemicals, shipyards, textiles, paper.

Wheat, cotton, gums, opium, fruit, rice, barley, sugar beets, tobacco, tea, corn, millet, legumes, vegetables, nuts; sheep, goats, cattle, asses, horses, mules; fish; petroleum oil, red oxide, copper, sulphur, arsenic, coal, salt, marble, nickel, manganese, lead, cobalt, turquoise, iron ore; carpets, textiles, leather, glass, matches, chemicals, jute, tobacco products, oil refining, casings, wood, oils.

Dates, other fruits, barley, wheat, rice, tobacco, cotton, beans, corn, sorghum, sesame; sheep, goats, asses, camels, horses, buffalo; petroleum; salt, wool, textiles, cigarettes, distilling, hides.

Hay, potatoes, turnips, beets, sugar beets, oats, wheat, bar-ley, rye, flax; cattle, sheep, pigs; fish; coal, peat, gypsum; tobacco, dairy products, foodstuffs, beer, malt, machinery, meats, textiles, boots and shoes, wood and paper products.

INDIA: A typical scene in one of the busy streets of the native section in Bombay.

TWA–Trans World Airlines

INDONESIA: Educational progress—a mother and daughter attending school together.

Indonesian Info. Office

POLITICAL DIVISION	GOVERNMENT	MONETARY UNIT	LANGUAGE	RELIGION
ISRAEL	Republic with president, prime minister, cabinet and elective unicameral legislature.	Israeli pound	Hebrew Arabic	Judaist Mohammedan Christian
ITALY	A republic with a president, a two-house, elective legislature and an appointive cabinet.	lira	Italian	Roman Cathol
IVORY COAST	One party republic of the French Community, with a president, cabinet, and a unicameral legislature.	CFA franc	Sudanese languages French	Tribal religion Mohammedan Christian
JAMAICA	Independent member of the British Commonwealth, with a governor-general, prime minister, cabinet, and bicameral legislature.	Jamaican pound (dollar-1969)	English	Protestant Roman Cathol
JAPAN	Constitutional monarchy with the executive power vested in prime minister and cabinet, the legislative power residing in a two-house parliament. The duties of the emperor are merely ceremonial.	yen	Japanese	Buddhist Shinto
JORDAN	Constitutional monarchy with cabinet and bicameral legislature.	Jordan dinar	Arabic	Mohammedan
KENYA	One party republic of the British Commonwealth, with a president, cabinet, and national assembly.	Kenya shilling	Bantu, Hamitic and Sudanese languages English; Swahili	Tribal religion Mohammedan Christian
KOREA	Divided by Armistice Line of August 1953: North Korea — a Communist "people's republic" ruled by the politburo; South Korea — a republic, with a president, cabinet, and a unicameral legislature.	won	Korean	Confucianist Buddhist Christian
KUWAIT	Constitutional sheikhdom, with a Sheikh, a cabinet and a unicameral national assembly.	Kuwaiti dinar	Arabic	Mohammedan
LAOS	Constitutional monarchy with a cabinet and a national assembly.	kip	Lao (Thai) French	Buddhist
LEBANON	Republic with a president, an appointed prime minister and cabinet, and an elected unicameral legislature.	Lebanese pound	Arabic French	Christian Mohammedan
LESOTHO	Kingdom with a king, prime minister, and a bicameral legislature.	South African rand	Sesotho English	Roman Cathol Protestant Tribal religion
LIBERIA	One party republic, with a president, cabinet, and a bicameral legislature.	Liberian dollar	English Sudanese languages	Christian Tribal religion Mohammedan
LIBYA	A kingdom with a prime minister, a cabinet and a bicameral legislature.	Libyan pound	Arabic	Mohammedan

MAJOR PRODUCTS

Dairy products, vegetables, eggs, fruits, wheat, hay, barley, corn, durra; goats, sheep, cattle, camels; fish; textiles, clothing, beverages, tobacco, diamond polishing, shoes, metal and woodwork, furniture, leather, dairy products, electrical products, paper, printing, false teeth, pharmaceuticals, chemicals, dyes, soap, radios, oil refining, wines.

Wheat, corn, oats, sugar beets, potatoes, tomatoes, rice, olives, grapes, lemons and other fruits, hemp, tobacco, nuts; fish; sheep and goats, cattle, pigs; iron ore, sulphur, zinc, bauxite, lead, mercury, marble, manganese; textiles, chemicals, wines, automobiles and machinery, electrical goods, beet sugar, olive oil, cheese, clothing, processed foods.

Coffee, cocoa, bananas, pineapples, corn, rice, kola, coconuts, palm oil, groundnuts, cotton, millet, tobacco; mahogany, caoutchouc; sheep, cattle, goats; diamonds, manganese.

Sugar cane, bananas, tobacco, coconuts, cacao, pimentoes, coffee, ginger; bauxite; honey; logwood; rum, textiles, cigars.

Rice, wheat, barley, mulberry trees, potatoes, sweet potatoes, fruits, rape, vegetables, oats, tobacco, soy beans, tea, flax, hemp, camphor; timber, bamboo; horses, cattle, sheep, goats, pigs, rabbits; fish, agar, pearl oysters; silkworms; coal, pyrites, gold, copper, pyrethrum, manganese, silver, sulphur, chromite, zinc, salt, tin, lead, iron, petroleum; textiles, steel, paper, porcelain, earthenware, lacquer ware, vegetable oil, toys, shoes, machinery, vehicles, electric goods, instruments.

Wheat, barley, legumes, vegetables, fruits, olives; sheep, goats, camels; salt, phosphate, potash; wool, tobacco products, flour milling, building materials, olive oil, leather goods.

Sisal, wheat, tea, coffee, pyrethrum, cotton, corn, sugar cane, sesame, groundnuts, wattle; hides and skins; timber; sodium carbonate, gold, kyanite, salt, silver, lime, bags, butter, sugar, sisal products, petroleum products.

Rice, barley, millet, wheat, soya beans, cotton, tobacco, hemp, ginseng, fruit; timber; draft cattle, pigs, sheep, fish; gold, iron ore, coal, tungsten, copper, silver, graphite, salt, kaolin, bismuth, fluorite, minerals (N. Korea); textiles, fertilizer, chemicals, cement, heavy industries (N. Korea); textiles, cement, silkworms, chemicals, machinery, metal, rubber, wood, paper and tobacco products (S. Korea).

Petroleum, shipbuilding (dhows), pearls, skins, wool, fish.

Rice, coffee, tea, citrus fruits, corn, cinchona, gum, benzoin, tobacco, cardamon; stick-lac; teak; tin; wool products.

Wheat, barley, corn, potatoes, fruits, onions, olives, tobacco; goats, asses, cattle, buffalo, sheep, horses, mules; iron, lignite; textiles, cement, olive oil, tobacco products, soap, matches, petroleum refining, gasoline, leather.

Corn, wheat, sorghum, barley, oats, beans, peas; cattle, sheep, goats, horses, donkeys, pigs, mules; diamonds; wool, mohair.

Rubber, rice, coffee, cassava, sugar cane, cacao, palm oil and kernels, piassava, groundnuts; rum; iron ore, diamonds.

Barley, wheat, olives, grapes, dates, almonds, figs, peanuts, citrus fruits, tobacco, esparto; goats, sheep, camels; sponge and tuna fishing; hides and skins; petroleum; matting, carpets, leather articles, embroidered fabrics, olive oil.

ITALY: A gondolier and his craft on one of the many waterways in Venice.

TWA–Trans World Airlines

LUXEMBOURG: La Place Guillaume, in the heart of the grand duchy's picturesque capital city.

Office Nat'l du Tourisme

Social and Economic Tables

POLITICAL DIVISION	GOVERNMENT	MONETARY UNIT	LANGUAGE	RELIGION
LIECHTENSTEIN	Principality, with an elected unicameral legislature.	Swiss franc	German	Roman Catholic
LUXEMBOURG	Constitutional grand duchy, with a minister of state, cabinet, council of state, and a unicameral legislature.	Luxembourg franc	Letzeburgisch (German dialect) French	Roman Catholic
MACAO	Portuguese overseas province ruled by a governor.	pataca	Chinese Portuguese	Confucianist Buddhist Taoist Christian
MALAGASY REPUBLIC	Republic of the French Community, with a president, cabinet, and a bicameral legislature.	Malagasy franc	French Malagasy and Bantu languages	Tribal religions Roman Catholic Protestant
MALAWI	Republic of the British Commonwealth, with president, cabinet, and a unicameral legislature.	Malawi pound	Bantu languages English	Tribal religions Protestant Roman Catholic
MALAYSIA	Independent federation of the British Commonwealth, with a head and a deputy head of state, a council of rulers, cabinet, and bicameral legislature.	Malaysian dollar	Malay English Chinese Indonesian languages Hindi, Tamil	Mohammedan Confucianist Tribal religions Buddhist Hindu Taoist
MALDIVE ISLANDS	Independent sultanate, with a prime minister and a unicameral legislature.	Celanese rupee	Maldivian English	Mohammedan
MALI	One party republic at present under a revolutionary committee and a consultative group. The president rules by decree.	Mali franc	Sudanese and Hamitic languages French	Mohammedan Tribal religions
MALTA	An independent member of the British Commonwealth, with a prime minister, a cabinet and a unicameral legislature.	Maltese pound	Maltese and English	Roman Catholic
MARTINIQUE	Overseas department of France with a prefect and elective general council.	French franc	Creole, French	Roman Catholic
MAURITANIA	One party republic of the French Community, with a president, cabinet, and a unicameral legislature.	CFA franc	French Arabic	Mohammedan
MAURITIUS	Independent member of the British Commonwealth, with a governor, premier, cabinet, and unicameral legislature.	Mauritius rupee	English Hindustani French	Roman Catholic Hindu Mohammedan
MEXICO	Federative republic with a president, council of ministers and a two-house legislature.	Mexican peso	Spanish	Roman Catholic
MONACO	Principality with elected national and communal councils.	French franc	French	Roman Catholic
MONGOLIA	Communist republic, ruled by chairman of the presidium of a unicameral legislature.	tughrik	Mongolian Kazakh	Lamaist Tribal religions
MOROCCO	Constitutional monarchy, with appointed prime minister and cabinet, and a bicameral legislature.	dirham	Arabic Berber French Spanish	Mohammedan Roman Catholic Jewish

of the World

MAJOR PRODUCTS

Grain, fruit, grapes, wood; cattle, pigs, chickens; cotton textiles, wine, leather, false teeth, pottery, wood-carving.

Oats, potatoes, wheat, rye, grapes; livestock; iron ore, slate, gypsum, sand and gravel; iron, steel and metal working; chemicals, non-metallic minerals, beverages, tobacco, leather, wines, dairy products, quarrying.

Fish; preserves, firecrackers, vegetable oil, cement, metal work, lumber, tobacco (processed), matches, wine.

Cassava, rice, corn, potatoes, vanilla, cloves, coffee, sugar cane, beans, groundnuts, sisal, castor oil, tobacco, raffia; timber; cattle, pigs, goats, sheep; graphite, mica, phosphates; textiles, sugar and rice factories, tapioca.

Tobacco, tea, cotton, pulses, tung oil, sisal, corn, sugar cane, cassava, wheat, rice, millet, groundnuts, rubber, beeswax, timber; goats, cattle, pigs, sheep; hides, skins, meat, ghee, soap; gold, mica, corundum.

Rubber, rice, coconuts, coffee, pineapples, pepper, sugar, tobacco, fibers, vegetables, tea; timber; buffalo, swine, oxen, goats; fish; tin, iron ore, bauxite, petroleum, antimony, manganese; copra, palm oil, timber, gold, rubber products, canning, shipping, milling, gasoline, wood products, textiles.

Coconuts, copra, coir, fruits, nuts; fish; cowries; cloth, mats, boats.

Millet, rice, sorghum, groundnuts, corn, sweet potatoes, gum arabic, cotton, manioc, tobacco, nuts, sisal; cattle, goats, sheep, horses, asses, camels; hides and skins; pottery, bricks, jewelry, weaving, leather, rice mills, soap.

Wheat, barley, potatoes, onions, grapes and other fruits, cumin seed, cotton; goats, sheep, pigs, cattle; fish; lace, filigree, wine, footwear, beer, cigarettes, buttons, pipes, gloves.

Sugar cane, cocoa, mangoes, avocados, pineapples, bananas, coffee; rum, sugar.

Millet, gum, dates, corn, watermelons, wheat, henna; sheep and goats, cattle, camels, asses, horses; hides and skins; fish; salt, iron ore.

Sugar, aloe fiber, rice, vanilla beans, hemp, sisal, groundnuts, tea, yams, manioc, pineapples, tobacco, coconuts; alcohol, molasses, rum, copra.

Corn, wheat, sugar, bananas, barley, cotton, coffee, vegetables; cattle; henequen; fish; silver, petroleum, lead, gold, zinc, copper; textiles, sugar, alcohol, foundry products, oil refining.

Principal revenue derived from Monte Carlo gambling casino. Tobacco, postage stamps, perfume, liqueurs, olive oil, oranges.

Stock raising (sheep, goats, cattle, horses, camels); milk, butter, cheese; wool, hides, skins, horns, bricks, machinery; coal, lead, gold.

Wheat, barley, olives, almonds, citrus fruits, dates, beans, grapes, vegetables, linseed; cork, cedar; hides & skins; timber; sheep, goats, cattle, asses, camels, horses; fish; phosphates, iron ore, anthracite, manganese, zinc, cobalt, antimony; leather, carpets, olive oil, wine, wool.

MEXICO: The Pyramid of the Sun at San Juan Teotihuacan, not far from Mexico City.

J. Walter Thompson

MOROCCO: Downtown Casablanca, the chief port, with the Place Lyautey in the foreground.

French Gov't Tourist Office

227

Social and Economic Tables

POLITICAL DIVISION	GOVERNMENT	MONETARY UNIT	LANGUAGE	RELIGION
MOZAMBIQUE	Portuguese overseas province ruled by a governor and a government council.	Portuguese escudo	Bantu languages Portuguese	Tribal religions Roman Catholic
MUSCAT AND OMAN	An independent sultanate.	Persian Gulf Indian rupee Maria Theresa dollar	Arabic Hindi	Mohammedan Hindu
NAURU	Republic with a president, cabinet, and legislative assembly.	Australian dollar	English Nauruan	Protestant
NEPAL	Constitutional monarchy, with cabinet, privy council, and a unicameral legislature.	Nepalese rupee	Nepali Hindi Tibetan	Hindu Buddhist Lamaist
NETHERLANDS	A constitutional, hereditary monarchy governed by the queen, her ministers and a two-house legislature, partly elective and partly chosen by provincial councils.	guilder	Dutch	Roman Catholic Protestant
NETHERLANDS ANTILLES	Self-governing part of Netherlands Union with governor, executive council and one-house legislature.	Dutch guilder	Dutch and Papiamento	Roman Catholic Protestant
NEW CALEDONIA	French overseas territory with a governor, a government council and a territorial assembly.	CFP franc	Melanesian dialects French	Roman Catholic Tribal religions
NEW GUINEA, TERR. OF	Australian U.N. trusteeship, governed jointly with Papua by an administrator, an administrative council and a house of assembly.	Australian dollar	Papuan Pidgin English English	Tribal religions Roman Catholic Protestant
NEW HEBRIDES	British and French condominium administered by British and French resident commissioners, with a partly elected advisory council.	Australian dollar New Hebrides franc	Melanesian dialects Pidgin English English French	Tribal religions Protestant Roman Catholic
NEW ZEALAND	An independent member of the British Commonwealth governed by a governor-general, a prime minister, a cabinet and a unicameral assembly.	New Zealand pound	English Maori	Protestant
NICARAGUA	Republic with a president, cabinet and a two-house legislature.	córdoba	Spanish	Roman Catholic
NIGER	One party republic of the French Community, with a president, cabinet, and unicameral legislature.	CFA franc	Sudanese Hamitic Arabic French	Mohammedan Tribal religions
NIGERIA	Federal republic of the British Commonwealth, at present under military rule, with a president, a supreme military council and a federal executive council.	Nigerian pound	Sudanese languages English	Mohammedan Christian Tribal religions
NIUE	New Zealand dependency, with a resident commissioner and a legislative assembly.	New Zealand dollar	Melanesian and Polynesian dialects; English	Protestant

of the World

MAJOR PRODUCTS

Sugar, corn, cotton, copra, sisal, cashew nuts, bananas, coffee, kapok, sorghum, manioc, tea, tobacco, vegetable oils; mangrove bark, timber; oxen, goats, pigs, sheep; gold, silver, asbestos, uranium, bauxite, samerskite.

Dates, pomegranates, limes and other fruits, tobacco, sugar cane; dried fish; petroleum.

Phosphates.

Rice, grains, jute, sugar cane, tea, vegetables, tobacco, cotton, potatoes, medicinal herbs; timber; cattle, hides, skins, ghee; iron, coal, copper, lead, zinc; cotton cloth, pottery, paper.

Potatoes, sugar beets, rye, wheat, oats, barley, flax, legumes, flower bulbs, seeds, vegetables, fruit; cattle, pigs, sheep, horses, poultry; fish; coal, petroleum, natural gas, salt; leather, rubber, footwear; metal products, textiles, paper, building materials, chemicals, foods and beverages, clothing, shipbuilding, cheese, fertilizers, ceramics, cement, tobacco products, petroleum products, machinery.

Fish; dividivi (tannin), crude salt, phosphates; refined petroleum.

Coconuts, copra, coffee, cotton, manioc, corn, tobacco, bananas, pineapples, wheat, rice, kauri logs; cattle, pigs, horses, goats, sheep, hides; guano, trochus shell; nickel, chrome, manganese, iron, cobalt, copper, lead, platinum; canned meat.

Coconuts, copra, cocoa, dairying, timber; gold, silver, platinum; boat making.

Coconuts, copra, cocoa, coffee, yams, taro, manioc, fruits; kauri pine; cattle, pigs; trochus shells.

Wheat, oats, barley, seeds, kauri, gum; sheep, cattle, pigs, horses; hides, skins; fish; gold, silver, coal, copper, limestone, manganese, iron, tungsten; dairy products, meats, wool, clothing, lumber, woodwork, furniture, electrical and radio goods, motor assembly, printing, publishing, biscuits, confections, footwear, rubber products, chemical fertilizers, tobacco products, brewing.

Coffee, sugar cane, sesame, corn, bananas, rice, cacao, cotton, beans; cattle; hardwoods; gold, copper, silver; sugar, wood products.

Millet, manioc, groundnuts, rice, wheat, cotton, gum arabic, kapok, kidney beans, corn, onions, sorghum, dates, sugar cane; goats, sheep, cattle, asses, camels, horses; hides and skins, leather; natron, sodium sulphate, salt, tin.

Palm oil and kernels, cacao, groundnuts, cotton, rubber, bananas, seeds, nuts, cassava, corn, rice, fruits, millet, coffee; cattle, sheep, goats; hides and skins; timber; tin, coal, columbite, gold, petroleum, zinc; cigarettes, soap, sugar.

Copra, sweet potatoes, bananas; hats, baskets.

NEW ZEALAND: Mt. Cook, the country's highest peak, and the Southern Alps are seen across Lake Matheson, on the South Island.

Nat'l Publicity Studios

NORWAY: The popular resort of Balestrand, on the Sogne Fjord in western Norway.

Scandinavian Travel Comm'n

Social and Economic Tables

POLITICAL DIVISION	GOVERNMENT	MONETARY UNIT	LANGUAGE	RELIGION
NORTHERN IRELAND	Executive power vested in appointed governor and cabinet responsible to legislative two-house parliament.	pound sterling	English	Protestant Roman Catholic
NORWAY	A constitutional, hereditary monarchy headed by the king, his council of state and a two-house, elective legislature.	krone (crown)	Norwegian	Protestant
PACIFIC ISLANDS, TRUST TERR.	United States U.N. trusteeship, with a high commissioner and a bicameral Congress of Micronesia.	American dollar	English Micronesian dialects	Roman Catholic Protestant
PAKISTAN	Independent republic within the British Commonwealth ruled by a president, cabinet and unicameral legislature.	Pakistani rupee	Urdu, Bengali, Pujabi, Pushtu, Sindhi, Baluchi English	Mohammedan Hindu
PANAMA	Republic with a president, two vice-presidents, a cabinet and a unicameral legislature.	balboa	Spanish	Roman Catholic
PAPUA	(For Government, see New Guinea, Terr. of)	Australian dollar	Papuan Pidgin English English	Tribal religions Protestant Roman Catholic
PARAGUAY	A centralized republic with a president, an appointed cabinet and a bicameral legislature.	guaraní	Spanish Indian (Guaraní)	Roman Catholic
PERU	A republic with a president, two vice-presidents, appointive cabinet and a two-house legislature.	sol	Spanish Indian (Quechua, Aymará)	Roman Catholic
PHILIPPINES	Republic governed by a president, cabinet and a bicameral legislature.	Philippine peso	Tagalog (Pilipino) English Spanish	Roman Catholic Mohammedan Tribal religions
PITCAIRN ISLANDS	British colony, with a chief magistrate under the governor of Fiji.	New Zealand dollar	English Tahitian	Seventh Day Adventist
POLAND	A Soviet-type "People's Republic" headed by a one-party legislative Sejm which elects an executive Council of Ministers. Actual power in the hands of politburo, highest organ of Communist party.	zloty	Polish	Roman Catholic
PORTUGAL	A "unitary corporative republic" with a president, premier, and a one-house elective legislature.	escudo	Portuguese	Roman Catholic
PORTUGUESE GUINEA	Portuguese overseas province ruled by a governor.	Portuguese escudo	Sudanese languages Portuguese	Tribal religions Roman Catholic
PORTUGUESE TIMOR	Portuguese overseas province ruled by a governor.	Portuguese escudo	Malay Portuguese	Mohammedan Tribal religions Roman Catholic

of the World

PERU: The beginning of festivities in the bull ring in Lima, the capital city.

Pan American World Airways

MAJOR PRODUCTS

Potatoes, oats, flax, turnips, hay; cattle, sheep, pigs; basalt and igneous rocks, sand and gravel; linen, rayon, woolen goods, carpets, hosiery, cotton goods, shirts, collars, shipbuilding, aircraft, machinery, rope, tobacco, whiskey.

Hay, potatoes, oats, barley, wheat, rye, fruits, vegetables; dairy products, livestock; fish; iron, copper, zinc, nickel, molybdenum; timber; pulp, cellulose, paper, canned foods, electro-chemical products, transportation equipment, salted, dried and canned fish, leather, textiles, fertilizers, shipbuilding, aluminum.

Copra, vegetables, fish, tropical fruits, coconuts, trochus shell; poultry, livestock.

Rice, wheat, corn, jute, cotton, sugar cane, fruit, oilseeds, tobacco, tea, fibers; timber; cattle, goats, sheep, horses, camels; hides, skins, wool; fish; salt, copper, petroleum, chromite, gypsum, limestone, natural gas, antimony; textiles, flour, cement, iron and steel, sugar, leather, chemicals, glass, sportsgoods, handicrafts, surgical instruments.

Bananas, cacao, abacá, coconuts, rice, sugar cane, coffee, pineapples; fish, shellfish, cattle; hardwoods; gold; hides, sugar, wood products, textiles, leather products.

Coconuts, rubber, sweet potatoes, yams, taro, sago, rice, bananas, coffee, kapok, bamboo, sisal hemp, copra; shells, sponges; cattle, goats, poultry; gold, copper, manganese.

Cotton, tobacco, sugar cane, rice, yerba maté, corn, coffee, citrus fruits; cattle, hides; lumber, quebracho; iron, manganese, copper; canned meats, vegetable oils, cigarettes.

Cotton, sugar, potatoes, barley, corn, rice, wheat, coca, quinoa, cacao, tobacco, coffee, quinine, flax, rubber, balata, guano; fish; livestock; petroleum, lead, zinc, copper, silver, gold, vanadium; textiles, foodstuffs, cement, leather, wool, hides, pharmaceuticals, paper products, clothing, metal.

Rice, sugar cane, copra, manila hemp (abacá), corn, tobacco, maguey, rubber, bananas, pineapples, mangoes, papaya, citrus fruits; hogs, carabaos, cattle, horses; fish; timber; gum resins, tan and dye barks; gold, iron, copper, chromite, silver, manganese, asbestos, asphalt, coal, petroleum; sugar, textiles, distilling, desiccated coconuts, tobacco products, rice milling, cocoa, coconut oil, embroideries.

Fruits, vegetables, goats, poultry; handicraft.

Potatoes, hay, rye, sugar beets, oats, barley, wheat, peas, beans, flax, hemp, rapeseed; livestock; fish; zinc, lead, coal, salt, iron ore, petroleum, natural gas, phosphates, lignite; iron and steel, coke, foods and beverages, textiles, cement, lime, bricks, electrical goods, chemicals, wood, timber, paper, cellulose, leather, leather products, glass.

Wheat, corn, oats, barley, rye, rice, beans, potatoes, grapes, olives; livestock; cork, lumber, resin; fish; copper pyrites, coal, copper, tin, kaolin, cement, wolfram, sulphur, tungsten, iron; wines, olive oil, canned sardines, textiles, porcelain, tiles, embroideries, lace, jute, machinery.

Rice, palm kernels and oil, wax, groundnuts; hides.

Coffee, copra, sandalwood, wax, cocoa; hides, shells.

PORTUGAL: The Praça dos Restauradores in Lisbon, with the monument dedicated to the seventeenth century restorers of Portuguese independence.

Photo "Sni-Yan"

Social and Economic Tables

POLITICAL DIVISION	GOVERNMENT	MONETARY UNIT	LANGUAGE	RELIGION
PUERTO RICO	Self-governing "free state" associated with the United States, with a governor, advisory council, and a bicameral legislature.	American dollar	Spanish, English	Roman Catholic
QATAR	British protected sheikhdom, advised by a political agent.	riyal	Arabic	Mohammedan
RÉUNION	French overseas department, with a prefect and general council.	French franc	French	Roman Catholic
RHODESIA	Self-governing British Commonwealth member, with a governor, prime minister, cabinet, and legislative assembly. Unilateral independence declared in 1965.	Rhodesian pound	Bantu languages English	Tribal religions Protestant
RUMANIA	A Soviet-type "People's Republic" with a president, a 17-member State Council, cabinet of ministers and a one-house legislature. Supreme power resides in Communist party politburo.	leu	Rumanian	Rumanian Orthodox
RWANDA	An independent republic with a president, a council of ministers and a legislative assembly.	Rwanda franc	Kinyarwanda Swahili French	Tribal religions Roman Catholic
RYUKYU IS.	U.S. administered, with a high commissioner, civil administrator and an elected local chief executive and unicameral legislature.	American dollar	Luchuan Japanese English	Shinto Animism Christian
ST. HELENA	British colony with a governor, advisory and executive councils.	pound sterling	English	Protestant
ST. PIERRE AND MIQUELON	French overseas territory with a governor, privy council and elective general council.	CFA franc	French	Roman Catholic
SAN MARINO	Republic with two regents, council of state, one-house legislature.	lira	Italian	Roman Catholic
SÃO TOMÉ AND PRÍNCIPE	Portuguese overseas province administered by a governor.	Portuguese escudo	Bantu languages Portuguese	Tribal religions Roman Catholic
SAUDI ARABIA	Absolute monarchy, with premier and cabinet responsible to the king and advisory councils.	riyal	Arabic	Mohammedan
SCOTLAND	A secretary of state for Scotland in the British cabinet has in his charge four departments for agriculture, education, health and home. Authority in other matters is exercised by other members of the British cabinet.	pound sterling	English and Gaelic	Protestant
SENEGAL	Republic in the French Community, with a president, cabinet, and unicameral legislature.	CFA franc	Sudanese languages French	Mohammedan Tribal religions Roman Catholic
SEYCHELLES	British colony with a governor and executive and legislative councils.	Mauritius rupee	English French	Roman Catholic
SIERRA LEONE	One party member of the British Commonwealth, with prime minister, cabinet and unicameral legislature, at present under a military junta.	leone	Sudanese languages English Creole	Tribal religions Mohammedan Christian

of the World

MAJOR PRODUCTS

Sugar cane, tobacco, fruits, pineapples, grapefruit, coconuts, coffee, cotton, livestock, vegetables; molasses, embroideries, rum, canned fruit and juice, alcohol, cordials, tobacco products.

Dates; pearl fishing, dried fish; camels; petroleum.

Sugar, rum, vanilla, tapioca, essences, fruit and vegetable preserves.

Corn, tobacco, groundnuts, wheat, potatoes, cotton, tea, sugar, citrus and other fruits; cattle, sheep, pigs, goats; meats, hides; copper, gold, asbestos, chromite, coal; footwear, apparel, cigarettes, flour, groundnut oil, wood products.

Wheat, barley, rye, corn, oats, potatoes, sugar beets, hemp, flax, grapes, fruits, tobacco; lumber; sheep, cattle, pigs, horses; petroleum, natural gas, salt, coal, lignite, iron and copper ores, gold, silver, bauxite, lead, manganese, zinc; flour, brewing and distilling, iron and steel, metal products, textiles, wood and paper products.

Coffee, cotton, tea, corn, groundnuts, vegetables; cattle, goats; hides; cassiterite, pyrethrum.

Sweet potatoes, sugar cane, rice, fruits, mulberries; swine, cattle, goats, horses, poultry; silkworms; fish; Panama hats, textiles, lacquer, pottery, china, glassware, tiles, plywood.

Hemp, lily bulbs, potatoes, tow, rope and twine, lace; sheep, goats, cattle, donkeys, poultry.

Fish, silver fox; dried cod and cod liver oil; sienna earth, yellow ocher.

Cattle, hides, wines, quarrying; textiles, tiles, ceramics.

Cacao, coffee, coconuts, copra, palm oil, cinchona, bananas.

Dates, sorghum, wheat, rice, henna, coffee, fruits, nuts, vegetables, gum, sesame oil; fish; camels, sheep, goats, cattle, donkeys, horses; hides, wool, butter, charcoal, pottery, salt, soap; petroleum, gold, pearls, copper, lead, silver.

Turnips, potatoes, wheat, barley, sugar beets, flax, vegetables, furits; sheep, cattle, horses; coal, iron ore, granite, sandstone, limestone, slate, lead, clay; steel, machinery, tools, locomotives, electronic equipment, linoleum, shipbuilding, watches, bagging, textiles, hosiery, thread, lace, carpet, yarn, chemicals, whiskey, paper, clay products, preserves, boots and shoes, furniture.

Millet, groundnuts, manioc, rice, corn, gum arabic, palm nuts, honey, sisal, indigo; sheep, goats, cattle; fish; titanium, phosphates; brick, pottery, weaving, jewelry, oil cakes.

Coconuts, cinnamon, patchouli, copra, vanilla, corn; guano; salted fish, tortoise shell, calipee.

Palm oil and kernels, coffee, kola nuts, ginger, piassava, groundnuts, cocoa; diamonds, iron ore, chrome ore.

PUERTO RICO: One of the island's chief products, pineapples, on their way to the cannery.

Hamilton Wright

SCOTLAND: Loch Garten, a highland lake in the eastern part of Inverness.

British Travel Ass'n

Social and Economic Tables

POLITICAL DIVISION	GOVERNMENT	MONETARY UNIT	LANGUAGE	RELIGION
SINGAPORE	Republic in the British Commonwealth, with a president, cabinet, and unicameral legislature.	Singapore dollar	Malay Chinese Tamil English	Confucianist Buddhist Taoist; Hindu Mohammedan Christian
SOLOMON ISLANDS	British protectorate, with high commissioner and executive and legislative councils.	Australian dollar	Melanesian Pidgin English English	Tribal religions Protestant Roman Catholic
SOMALI REPUBLIC	Republic with a president, prime minister, cabinet, and a unicameral legislature.	Somali shilling	Somali; Arabic Italian English	Mohammedan
SOUTH AFRICA	Republic with a state president, prime minister, executive council and bicameral legislature.	rand	Afrikaans English Bantu languages Bushman	Protestant Roman Catholic Mohammedan Hindu Buddhist
SOUTHERN YEMEN	Republic with president and cabinet.	South Arabian dinar	Arabic	Mohammedan
SOUTH-WEST AFRICA	Mandated to South Africa, now governed by an administrator and legislative assembly, with representation in the South African legislature.	South African rand	Afrikaans English; German Bantu languages Bushman	Tribal religions Protestant Roman Catholic
SPAIN	A nominal monarchy governed by a chief of state. The legislative Cortés prepares laws subject to the veto of the chief of state. A king is to be chosen by a regency council upon the death or incapacitation of the chief of state.	peseta	Spanish Catalan	Roman Catholic
SPANISH SAHARA	Overseas Spanish province, with a high commissioner, cabinet and a unicameral legislature.	Spanish peseta	Arabic Spanish	Mohammedan
SUDAN	Republic at present under a council of state, nominally aided by a premier and an assembly.	Sudanese pound	Arabic Sudanese and Hamitic languages English	Mohammedan Tribal religions Christian
SURINAM	Self-governing part of the Netherlands Union, with governor, ministerial, advisory, and legislative councils.	Netherlands Antilles guilder	Dutch	Christian Moslem Hindu
SWAZILAND	Monarchy within the British Commonwealth, with a prime minister, cabinet and bicameral legislature.	South African rand	Bantu languages English Afrikaans	Tribal religions Christian missions
SWEDEN	A constitutional hereditary monarchy with a prime minister, council of state and a two-house elective legislature.	krona (crown)	Swedish	Protestant
SWITZERLAND	A republic with a president, vice-president, an executive federal council and a two-house, elective legislature.	Swiss franc	German French Italian Romansch	Protestant Roman Catholic

of the World

MAJOR PRODUCTS

Rubber, coconuts, fruits, vegetables, rice, coffee, tapioca, tobacco, sweet potatoes, pepper, pineapples; pigs, poultry, cattle; fish; tin; tin smelting, rubber milling, coconut milling, soap, beer, pineapple canning, biscuits, brick making, shipping, textiles, palm oil, cigarettes, gasoline, kerosene.

Copra, pigs, poultry; trochus shell, turtle shell, bêche-de-mer.

Sugar, cotton, tobacco, bananas, aromatic gums, resin, kapok, grains, beans; camels, goats, sheep, cattle; skins, hides; tunny, mother-of-pearl.

Corn, wheat, potatoes, oats, kaffir-corn, barley, tobacco, sugar cane, tea, citrus fruits, rye, groundnuts, grapes, pineapples; cattle, sheep, goats, pigs, horses, donkeys, mules; gold, coal, diamonds, copper, asbestos, manganese, lime, limestone, platinum, chrome, iron, silver, tungsten, mercury, vanadium, tin, antimony, silver, uranium, talc; hides, chemicals, wool, footwear, rubber, machinery, clothing, textiles, food, vehicles, printing, furniture, building materials, steel.

Dates, gums, tobacco, salt, fish oil, butter; wheat, barley, sesame, millet, sorghum, aloes, ghee; goats, sheep, camels, cattle; dhow building, ship bunkering.

Cattle, donkeys, horses, pigs; karakul; fish; diamonds, copper, lead, zinc, salt, tin, manganese, germanium.

Wheat, barley, potatoes, oranges, olives, oats, rye, rice, corn, peas, beans, grapes, onions, sugar beets, esparto, flax, hemp, pulse, cork, nuts; livestock and poultry; fish; coal, lignite, iron ore, lead, iron pyrites, potash, zinc, mercury, sulphur, copper; textiles, wines, olive oil, paper, cement, hides, leather, chemicals, machinery, vehicles, iron and steel, furniture.

Barley, corn; goats, sheep, camels; fish.

Cotton, cotton seed, gum arabic, Senna leaves and pods, groundnuts, sesame, millet, dates, dom nuts (vegetable ivory), wheat, shea nuts; sheep, goats, cattle, camels, asses; mahogany; hides and skins, ivory, gold, salt, trochus shell, mother-of-pearl.

Rice, citrus fruits, coconuts, coffee, bananas, sugar cane, cacao, balata, corn, tobacco; lumber; gold, bauxite; sugar, rum, plywood, molasses.

Tobacco, corn, groundnuts, kaffir-corn, sugar cane, wheat, oats, rye, barley; cotton, rice, fruits; cattle, goats, sheep, pigs; timber; butter; hides, skins; asbestos, gold, tin, iron.

Hay, sugar beets, potatoes, oats, wheat, rye, barley; forest products; cattle, pigs, sheep, horses; fish; iron ore, sulphur, arsenic, zinc, copper, silver, gold, lead, manganese; wood products, machinery, textiles, iron and steel, metal goods, chemicals, dairy products, tobacco products, porcelain, glass, shipbuilding, matches.

Wheat, potatoes, sugar beets, rye, oats, barley, fruits, tobacco; livestock; salt, iron, manganese; dairy products, textiles, watches and clocks, chemicals, foods, wines, dyes, drugs, machinery.

SOUTH AFRICA: Commissioner Street, in the downtown part of Johannesburg, the country's largest city.
South African Gov't Info. Office

SWITZERLAND: Milk still being delivered by dog cart in a rural section of the republic.
TWA—Trans World Airlines

Social and Economic Tables

POLITICAL DIVISION	GOVERNMENT	MONETARY UNIT	LANGUAGE	RELIGION
SYRIA	Officially the Syrian Arab Republic, with a president and cabinet, under a revolutionary council.	Syrian pound	Arabic Turkish Kurdish	Mohammedan Christian
TANZANIA	United republic within the British Commonwealth, with a president, two vice-presidents, cabinet, and two national assemblies (Tanganyika and Zanzibar).	Tanzanian shilling	Bantu languages English Arabic Swahili Gujarati	Tribal religions Mohammedan Christian missions
THAILAND (SIAM)	Constitutional monarchy, with a prime minister, council and a bicameral legislature.	baht	Thai Khmer	Buddhist Mohammedan Confucianist
TOGO	Republic of the French Community, with a president and a council of ministers.	CFA franc	Sudanese languages French	Tribal religions Mohammedan Roman Catholic
TOKELAU ISLANDS	An island territory of New Zealand with a high commissioner.	New Zealand dollar	Samoan	Protestant Roman Catholic
TONGA	British protected autonomous constitutional monarchy, with a privy council, cabinet and unicameral legislature. Independence sought.	pa'anga	Tongan English	Protestant Roman Catholic
TRINIDAD AND TOBAGO	Independent British Commonwealth member, with prime minister, cabinet, and a bicameral legislature.	Trinidad and Tobago dollar	English	Roman Catholic Protestant Hindu; Moslem
TRUCIAL OMAN	Seven sheikhdoms under British protection with a British agent.	riyal	Arabic	Mohammedan
TUNISIA	A republic with a president, a cabinet of secretaries of state, and an assembly.	Tunisian dinar	Arabic French Berber	Mohammedan Roman Catholic
TURKEY	Republic with a president, prime minister, cabinet, and a bicameral legislature.	Turkish pound (lira)	Turkish Kurdish Arabic	Mohammedan
UGANDA	Republic of the British Commonwealth, with a president, vice-president, cabinet and assembly.	Uganda shilling	Sudanese, Bantu, Hamitic languages English	Tribal religions Christian
U.S.S.R.	A federation of 15 socialist republics with a two-chamber legislative assembly (Supreme Soviet) which elects the executive presidium and council of ministers. The policy of the state is largely defined by the Central Committee of the Communist party, the only legal party.	ruble	Russian, Ukrainian, White Russian, Uzbek, Tatar, Azerbaidzhani, Georgian, Lithuanian, Armenian, Yiddish, Latvian, Mordvinian, Chuvash, Tadzhik, Estonian, Kazakh, etc.	Russian Orthodox Moslem
UNITED ARAB REP. (EGYPT)	Republic with a president (with supreme powers), cabinet, and elected unicameral legislature.	Egyptian pound	Arabic	Mohammedan Christian minorities
UNITED KINGDOM	See: England and Wales, Northern Ireland, Scotland.			

of the World

MAJOR PRODUCTS

Wheat, barley, sorghum, corn, cotton, vegetables, olives, grapes, tobacco; sheep, goats, cattle, camels, horses; wool, hides, skins; gypsum; leather, textiles, cement, wine, flour.

Sisal, cotton, cloves, coffee, bananas, tobacco, papain, vegetables, nuts, tea, oil seeds, beeswax, grains, sugar; cattle, goats, sheep; hides, skins; wood, timber, wax, gum arabic; diamonds, gold, mica, salt, camphor, tungsten, lead, silver; cement, textiles, petroleum products.

Rice, rubber, coconuts, sugar cane, tobacco, cotton, corn, beans; teak and other woods; bullocks, buffalo, horses, elephants; fish; tin, wolfram; lac, jute.

Palm oil and kernels, tapioca, cocoa, yams, coffee, plantains, corn, groundnuts, cotton, copra, kola, cassava, rubber; sheep, goats, pigs, cattle, asses, horses; phosphates.

Coconuts, fiber, taro, copra; pigs, chickens; fish; hats, mats.

Copra, bananas, fungus, candlenuts; pigs, cattle, goats.

THAILAND: The heroine and hero in costume for a classical dance in the Asian kingdom.

Gov't of Thailand

Coffee, cocoa, sugar cane, citrus fruits; cattle; petroleum, asphalt; rum, canned grapefruit juice, sugar, chemicals, textiles, plastic products.

Dates, grains, vegetables; fishing, pearl fishing.

Wheat, barley, oats, corn, sorghum, beans, grapes, olives, nuts, citrus fruits, dates, oranges, cork; sheep, goats, cattle, horses, asses, camels; fish, sponges; flour milling, oil refining, wine, olive oil, wool spinning, pottery, leather, silk weaving; phosphates, iron ore, lead, silver.

Tobacco, cereals, olives, cotton, figs, nuts, fruits; cattle, livestock; fish; chromium, iron ore, copper, coal, lignite, meerschaum, manganese; textiles, iron and steel, paper, rugs, olive oil, cement, petroleum products.

Cotton, coffee, tea, plantains, sisal, groundnuts, millet, cotton seed, tobacco, chilies, sugar cane, rubber; cattle, sheep, goats; hides, skins; copper, gold, phosphates, tin; cigarettes.

Wheat, rye, oats, barley, corn, sugar beets, sunflower seeds, cotton, forage crops, flax, hemp, potatoes, tobacco; cattle, sheep, goats, pigs, horses; lumber, furs; fish; coal, peat, petroleum, iron, lignite, copper, lead, zinc, nickel, aluminum, phosphates, manganese, gold, sulphur, potash, asbestos, platinum, salt, chromite; steel, machinery, textiles, sugar, flour, meats, automobiles, paper, synthetic rubber, foods, wines, chemicals.

Cotton, barley, wheat, rice, sugar cane, onions, oil seeds, corn, millet, fruits, vegetables; sheep, goats, cattle, buffalo, camels; fish; petroleum, cement, phosphates, salt, manganese, asbestos, chromite; cotton ginning, milling, pottery, perfume, soap, iron and steel.

TURKEY: The Galata Bridge, spanning the Golden Horn in Istanbul, one of the most heavily traveled bridges in the world.

Turkish Info. Office

Social and Economic Tables

POLITICAL DIVISION	GOVERNMENT	MONETARY UNIT	LANGUAGE	RELIGION
UNITED STATES	Federal republic with a president, vice-president and two-house legislature (senate and house of representatives), and an appointed cabinet. It consists of 50 states, each with a governor and state legislature.	American dollar	English	Protestant Roman Catholic Judaist
UPPER VOLTA	One party republic of the French Community, at present under a president ruling by decree, and a military dominated council.	CFA franc	Sudanese languages French	Tribal religions Mohammedan
URUGUAY	A republic governed by a National Council, an appointed cabinet and a two-house elective legislature.	Uruguayan peso	Spanish	Roman Catholic
VATICAN CITY	The Pope, elected for life by cardinals of the Roman Catholic Church, exercises absolute legislative, executive and judicial power. He appoints a governor of the state.	Italian lira	Italian Latin	Roman Catholic
VENEZUELA	A republic with a president, appointive cabinet, and elective two-house legislature.	bolívar	Spanish	Roman Catholic
VIETNAM	Divided in two parts by Armistice Line Sept. 1954. North of 17th parallel is Communist controlled "republic." South is a republic with a president and a bicameral legislature.	South: piastre North: dong	Vietnamese Khmer Lao French	Taoist Buddhist Confucianist Roman Catholic
VIRGIN ISLANDS (BR.)	British colony with an administrator, an executive and a legislative council.	B.W.I. dollar	English Creole	Protestant
VIRGIN ISLANDS (U.S.)	U.S. territory with an appointed governor, local executive departments and a local unicameral legislature.	American dollar	English Creole	Roman Catholic Protestant
WESTERN SAMOA	Independent state, with a head of state, prime minister, cabinet and unicameral legislature.	Western Samoa pound	Samoan English	Protestant Tribal religions
WEST IRIAN	Indonesian administered with independence due before 1969, ruled by a governor and a legislative assembly.	West Irian rupiah	Indonesian Papuan	Tribal religions
YEMEN	Under interim rule with rival royal and republican factions in control of parts of the country.	riyal	Arabic	Mohammedan
YUGOSLAVIA	A Soviet-type republic combining six republics under a central government with a president, fed. executive council and two-house elective legislature. Actually ruled by Communist League.	Yugoslav dinar	Serbian-Croatian Slovenian Macedonian	Eastern Orthodox Roman Catholic Mohammedan
ZAMBIA	Independent republic within the British Commonwealth, with a president, a cabinet and a unicameral legislature.	kwacha	Bantu languages English	Tribal religions

of the World

MAJOR PRODUCTS

Corn, hay, tobacco, wheat, cotton, oats, soy beans, potatoes, barley, sorghums, peanuts, rye, rice, citrus fruits, fruits, sugar beets, sugar cane, vegetables, tree nuts, feed grains and hay; livestock; fish; lumber; petroleum, coal, cement, iron, natural gas, copper, sand and gravel, zinc, lead, stone, gold, silver, molybdenum, bauxite, phosphates, mica, sulphur; foods, transportation equipment, machinery, primary metal products, electrical machinery, textiles, chemicals, paper and wood products, beverages, dairy products.

Millet, groundnuts, corn, karite nuts and butter (shea nut), vegetables, rice, tapes, cotton, kapok, sesame, sorghum, tea; sheep, goats, cattle, asses, pigs; gold, manganese, copper, silver, chrome, lignite, iron; hides and skins.

Wheat, corn, oats, seeds, peanuts, barley, rice, citrus fruits, peaches, grapes, vegetables, tobacco; sheep, cattle; gold; meat, hides, wool, textiles, leather, shoes, wines, chemicals.

UNITED STATES: The American Falls at Niagara Falls, New York, a major tourist attraction.
N.Y. State Dep't of Commerce

Coffee, cacao, sugar cane, corn, rice, cotton, tobacco, coconuts, beans, bananas, rubber; livestock; fish, pearls; petroleum, iron, gold, coal, copper, phosphates, nickel, asphalt, salt, diamonds; textiles, leather, sugar, cement, wood products, chemicals, vehicles, food products, meats; refined petroleum.

Rice, corn, sugar, tobacco, coffee, fruits, nuts, tea, cotton, medicinal plants, soya, rubber, copra, groundnuts, sweet potatoes, cinnamon; bamboo; silk; cattle, buffalo, pigs; lumber; gold, tin, copper, coal, zinc, iron, cement, limestone, calamine, tungsten, manganese, phosphate, lead, bauxite; paper, textiles, chemicals, cement, sugar.

Poultry and livestock, fish, fruit, vegetables.

Vegetables, citrus fruits, coconuts; cattle; fish; rum, bay rum, bay oil, molasses, handicrafts, sugar, lime juice, hides, bitters.

Copra, cocoa beans, bananas, taro; fish; pigs, poultry.

Sago, coconuts, sweet potatoes, wild nutmeg, mace, copra; bird of paradise plumes; petroleum.

Coffee, barley, wheat, millet, sesame; cattle, hides; fish.

Wheat, barley, rye, oats, corn, sugar beets, hemp, hops, opium, tobacco, flax, alfalfa, vegetables, fruits; sheep, cattle, pigs, goats, horses, poultry; coal, lignite, iron, copper, lead, salt, zinc, mercury, antimony, petroleum, bauxite, chrome, cement; lumber, textiles, foods, beverages, sugar, wood-distillates, wines, machinery, chemicals, shipbuilding.

Corn, wheat, potatoes, tobacco, sorghum, millet, groundnuts, cassava, rice, beans, cowpeas, cotton; lumber; cattle; copper, lead, manganese, zinc, cobalt, tin.

VENEZUELA: Avenida Bolívar and the thirty story office buildings of downtown Caracas.
Hamilton Wright

ECUADOR: Independence Plaza in Quito, with the Cathedral, the center of tourist activity in the country.

Hamilton Wright

ENGLAND: Trafalgar Square and the famous pillar dedicated to Lord Nelson, in London.

British Info. Services

AUSTRALIA: A view of Sydney Harbour, with the botanical gardens at Farm Cove in the foreground.

Qantas

INDIA: The Hawa Mahal at Jaipur, in the state of Rajasthan, with old and new forms of transportation.

Gov't of India Info. Bur.

TRINIDAD & TOBAGO: A typical mosque in Port of Spain.

Trinidad & Tobago Tourist Board

This alphabetical list of cities and towns gives statistics of population based on the latest official census reports or most re-
reliable estimates. Each line begins with the name of a place, followed by the name of the country or state, the population,
index reference and plate number. This index reference gives the location of the city or town name on the accompanying
plates. The name is found within the square formed by the two lines of latitude or longitude which enclose each of the co-
nates—i.e. the marginal letters and numbers. In the case of maps consisting entirely of insets, the name is found near the
rsection point of imaginary lines connecting the co-ordinates.

Where space on the map has not permitted giving the complete form of a name, the extended form is shown in the index.
re a place may be known under different names or by various spellings of the same name, the different forms have been included,
large extent, in the index. Where an alternative spelling in parentheses is shown on the map itself, the first name gives the
official form, the conventional form following in parentheses.

* Capitals of countries, states and provinces.   † Population figure includes suburbs or subdivision.

enraa, Denmark, 14,680	F 9 19	Aleppo, Syria, 562,753 ....G 4 46	An Nasiriya, Iraq, 60,405 ....E 3 44
en, Germany, 176,808 ......A 3 23	Alessandria, Italy, 65,908 ....B 2 28	Annecy, France, 42,304 ....G 5 25
org, Denmark, 85,128 ....G 8 19	Alexandretta (Iskenderun),	Anniston, Ala., 33,657 ....G 3 104
t, Belgium, 45,900 ....C 6 20	Turkey, 69,259 ....G 4 46	Annonay, France, 12,559 ....F 5 25
us, Denmark, 117,010 ....F 8 19	Alexandria, U.A.R., 1,800,951 ....M 5 63	Anshan, China, 833,000 ....K 3 51
dan, Iran, 302,189 ....E 3 44	Alexandria, La., 40,279 ....E 4 134	Antâkya, Turkey, 57,584 ....G 4 46
eville, France, 21,744 ....D 2 24	Alexandria, Va., 91,023 ....L 3 185	Antalya, Turkey, 71,632 ....D 4 46
cher, Chad, 25,000 ....L 9 63	Al Falluja, Iraq, 38,072 ....D 3 44	Antibes, France, 24,730 ....G 6 25
okuta, Nigeria, 187,292 ......G10 62	Algeciras, Spain, 51,096 ....D 4 26	Antofagasta, Chile, 112,421 ......F 8 70
rdare, Wales, 58,450 ....E 5 17	Algiers,* Algeria, 943,142 ....G 4 62	Antsirabe, Malagasy Rep.,
dare, Scotland, 183,463 ......E 2 16	Alhambra, Calif., 54,807 ....C10 113	26,947 ....R16 65
djan,* Ivory Coast, 285,000....E10 62	Alicante, Spain, 103,289 ....F 3 27	Antung, China, 370,000 ....K 3 51
ene, Tex., 90,368 ....E 5 180	Aligarh, India, 208,167 ....D 3 48	Antwerp (Antwerpen), Belgium,
(Turku), Finland, 139,141....N 6 19	Aliquippa, Pa., 26,369 ....B 4 172	241,154 ....D 5 20
mbaro, Mexico, 26,187 ....J 7 81	Alkmaar, Netherlands, †49,561....E 2 20	Anyang, China, 153,000 ....H 4 51
oulco, Mexico, 49,149 ....J 8 81	Al Kuwait,* Kuwait, 99,609 ......E 4 44	Anzhero-Sudzhensk, U.S.S.R.,
ra,* Ghana, 484,783 ....G10 62	Allahabad, India, 465,128 ....E 3 48	118,000 ....J 4 38
rrington, England, 37,470 ......G 1 16	Allentown, Pa., 108,347 ....L 4 173	Aomori, Japan, 224,433 ....F 2 52
e, Israel, 28,100 ....C 2 47	Alleppey, India, 150,866 ....D 7 49	Apeldoorn, Netherlands,
na, Turkey, 290,515 ....F 4 46	Alma-Ata, U.S.S.R., 636,000 ......L 5 42	†116,548 ....G 3 20
pazarı, Turkey, 85,579 ....D 2 46	Almelo, Netherlands, †57,722 ....J 3 20	Apia,* Western Samoa, 21,699....J 7 56
is Ababa,* Ethiopia,	Almería, Spain, 76,643 ....E 4 27	Apolda, Germany, 29,735 ....D 3 23
20,000 ....O10 63	Alor Star, Malaysia, 52,915 ......C 6 53	Appleton, Wis., 48,411 ....J 7 187
laide,* South Australia,	Altenburg, Germany, 47,462 ......E 3 23	'Aqaba, Jordan, 8,908 ....D 5 47
726,930 ....D 7 58	Alton, Ill., 43,047 ....A 6 125	Aracaju, Brazil, 112,516 ....N 6 69
n, Southern Yemen, 150,000....E 7 44	Altona, Germany, 260,275 ....C 2 22	Araçatuba, Brazil, 53,363 ....K 8 69
wa, Ethiopia ....O 9 63	Altoona, Pa., 69,407 ....F 4 172	Arad, Rumania, 126,005 ....E 2 34
on, Turkey, 43,646 ....D 3 46	Altrincham, England, 41,070 ......G 2 16	Aragua de Barcelona, Ven.,
ña,* Guam, 1,642 ....E 4 56	Amadora, Portugal, 36,331 ....A 1 26	8,241 ....H 2 68
n, France, 30,639 ....D 5 25	Amagasaki, Japan, 500,990 ......E 4 52	Arak, Iran, 58,998 ....E 3 44
a, India, 530,548 ....C 3 48	'Amara, Iraq, 64,847 ....E 3 44	Araraquara, Brazil, 58,076 ....L 8 69
igento, Sicily, Italy, 46,947......D 6 29	Amarillo, Tex., 137,969 ....C 2 180	Archangel, U.S.S.R., 308,000 ......F 2 36
ínion, Greece, 24,763 ....E 6 35	Ambala, India, 85,927 ....D 2 48	Ardebil, Iran, 65,742 ....E 2 44
ascalientes, Mexico, 152,293...H 6 80	Ambato, Ecuador, 53,372 ....E 4 68	Arequipa, Peru, †135,358 ....F 7 68
en, Germany, 44,775 ....B 3 22	Amboina (Ambon), Indon.,	Argentan, France, 11,724 ....D 3 24
nadabad, India,	56,037 ....H 6 55	Argenteuil, France, 82,007 ....A 1 24
316,223 ....C 4 48	Amecameca, Mexico, 12,291 ......M 1 81	Arica, Chile, 43,344 ....F 7 68
nadnagar, India, 126,353 ....C 5 49	Amersfoort, Netherlands,	Arles, France, 29,251 ....F 6 25
vaz, Iran, 155,054 ....E 3 44	†75,312 ....F 3 20	Arlington, Va., 163,401 ....L 3 185
, France, 55,398 ....F 6 25	Amiens, France, 101,677 ....E 3 24	Armavir, U.S.S.R., 134,000 ....F 5 37
-les-Bains, France, 17,324 ....G 5 25	Amman,* Jordan, 330,000 ....D 4 47	Armentières, France, 23,168 ......E 2 24
uwakamatsu, Japan, 102,239....F 2 57	Amoy, China, 308,000 ....J 7 51	Arnhem, Netherlands,
ccio,* Corsica, France,	Amravati, India, 156,579 ....D 4 49	†134,921 ....H 4 20
0,829 ....B 7 25	Amritsar, India, 403,255 ....C 2 48	Arras, France, 40,969 ....E 2 24
ner, India, 249,699 ....C 3 48	Amsterdam,* Neth., †943,667 ....E 3 20	Artigas, Uruguay, 17,684 ....J10 71
shi, Japan, 159,299 ....E 4 52	Amsterdam, N.Y., 28,772 ....M 5 161	Aš, Czechoslovakia, 10,000 ....B 1 32
isar, Turkey, 47,422 ....C 3 46	Ancona, Italy, 77,748 ....D 3 28	Asahikawa, Japan, 245,246 ....F 2 52
ta, Japan, 216,607 ....E 3 52	Anchorage, Alaska, 44,237 ....J 2 107	Asansol, India, 117,874 ....F 4 48
la, India, 129,707 ....D 4 49	Anderlecht, Belgium, 102,189......D 6 20	Aschaffenburg, Germany,
on, Ohio, 290,351 ....G 3 166	Anderson, Ind., 49,061 ....F 4 126	55,045 ....C 4 23
yubinsk, U.S.S.R., 131,000 ......F 6 38	Andheri, India, 122,401 ....B 8 49	Aschersleben, Germany,
ab, Burma, 42,329 ....A 2 53	Andizhan, U.S.S.R., 164,000 ......H 5 38	36,777 ....D 3 22
juela, Costa Rica,	Andorra la Vella,* Andorra,	Asheville, N.C., 60,192 ....E 8 162
9,620 ....E 6 78	2,250 ....G 1 27	Ashkhabad, U.S.S.R.,
meda, Calif., 61,316 ....J 2 112	Andria, Italy, 69,499 ....F 4 29	230,000 ....F 6 38
acete, Spain, 61,635 ....F 3 27	Angarsk, U.S.S.R., 179,000 ......L 4 39	Ashland, Ky., 31,283 ....M 4 133
any,* N.Y., 129,726 ....N 5 161	Angers, France, 109,614 ....C 4 24	Ashqelon, Israel, 28,400 ....B 4 47
any, Western Australia,	Angmagssalik, Greenland, 721 ....C11 10	Ashton, England, 49,050 ....G 2 16
1,417 ....B 6 58	Angora (Ankara),* Turkey,	Asmara, Ethiopia, 131,800 ....O 9 63
i, France, 31,672 ....E 6 25	†902,218 ....E 3 46	Asnières, France, 81,747 ....A 1 24
uquerque, N. Mex.,	Angoulême, France, 46,924 ......D 5 25	Asti, Italy, 44,455 ....B 2 28
01,189 ....C 3 158	Ankara,* Turkey,	Astrakhan', U.S.S.R.,
oy, Spain, 48,712 ....F 3 27	†902,218 ....E 3 46	361,000 ....G 5 37
ershot, England, 36,080 ....F 5 17	Anking, China, 129,000 ....J 5 51	Asunción,* Paraguay,
ridge-Brownhills, England,	Annaba, Algeria, 168,790 ....H 4 62	350,000 ....J 3 71
4,780 ....G 3 16	An Najaf, Iraq, 128,096 ....D 3 44	Aswân, U.A.R., 48,393 ....N 7 63
grete, Brazil, 33,735 ....J 9 71	Annapolis,* Md., 23,385 ....H 5 139	Asyût, U.A.R., 137,000 ....N 6 63
nçon, France, 24,299 ....D 3 24	Ann Arbor, Mich., 67,340 ....F 6 143	Atbara, Sudan, 36,298 ....N 8 63